French

verb handbook

Kate Dobson

D1510957

Berlitz Publishing Company, Inc.

Princeton   Mexico City   London   Eschborn   Singapore

French Verb Handbook

Reprinted September 2000
Printed in Canada
ISBN 2-8315-6388-7

The Author:
Kate Dobson is an experienced teacher at the primary school, high school, and adult level.

Series Editor:
Christopher Wightwick is a former UK representative on the Council of Europe Modern Languages Project and principal Inspector of Modern Languages for England.

CONTENTS

How to use this handbook

This Handbook aims to provide a full description of the French verb system for all learners and users of the French language. It provides the following information:

- a chapter on the verb system;
- the conjugation in full of sixty-one common verbs, grouped to show the common patterns underlying the system;
- a full subject index;
- a verb index containing over 2,200 verbs with their English meanings.

An important feature of the Handbook is that examples, showing many of the verbs in use, are given in the model verb pages.

Verbs in French: their functions and uses

This section describes the functions of verbs in general. Information is given on word order, the use of tenses, the way verbs govern different cases and prepositions, and the way they are formed.

Model French verbs

This section gives the conjugation in full of every tense of a verb. The reflexive verb form is also illustrated. Fifty-six common verbs are then set out as models.

A selection of verbs that follow the same pattern as each individual verb is listed underneath. Examples are then provided of these verbs in use, to illustrate different tenses and a wide range of different meanings and idiomatic constructions.

The subject index

The subject index gives paragraph references for all the main grammatical terms used.

The verb index

For each verb, information is given on whether it is transitive or intransitive, the auxiliary it takes in the past tenses, the prepositions that it governs, and its English meaning. Common secondary meanings are illustrated in a brief phrase. The most important and up-to-date forms of verbs are listed.

How to find the information you want

If you want to check on the form, meaning, or use of a verb, first look it up in the index. This gives a range of information:

• Any preposition that normally follows the verb.
• Whether the verb is transitive, intransitive, reflexive, or impersonal, and whether it takes the auxiliary **être** in the compound past tenses. If no auxiliary is shown, the verb takes **avoir**.
• The English meaning of the verb. Only the basic meaning is shown for most verbs.
• A number indicating on which model verb page or pages you will find further information about the verb or others like it.
• A short phrase or sentence following some verbs, giving important subsidiary meanings.

If you want further information on the form or use of the verb, turn to the model verb reference given. On these pages you will find:

• the full conjugation of the present, perfect, imperfect, and simple past of each model verb;
• the first person singular form of other tenses;
• a list of other verbs following the same pattern;
• notes indicating any exceptions to this pattern;
• short dialogues and sentences illustrating some of the different tenses and usages of these verbs.

If you want to know the full form of other tenses you should note that they are always regular. They can easily be checked by looking up the full tense of the relevant verb:

• **marcher** [➤1] a regular **-er** verb taking **avoir**;
• **tomber** [➤2] a regular **-er** verb taking **être**;
• **se laver** [➤3] a regular reflexive **-er** verb;
• **finir** [➤16] a regular **-ir** verb;
• **vendre** [➤28] a regular **-re** verb.

For further information on how the verb system works, refer to PART A, "Verbs in French: their functions and uses."

A
VERBS IN FRENCH:
THEIR FUNCTIONS AND USES

For a full treatment of this topic, see Berlitz *French Grammar Handbook.*

What do verbs do?

1a Full verbs

"Full" verbs in French do the same job as in English: that is, they communicate the action or feeling state or changing state of the subject. Their position in the sentence is similar to English word order:

Subject (noun or pronoun) – verb – rest of sentence

Mon frère a bu tout le champagne.	My brother has drunk all the champagne.
Il aime le vin rouge aussi.	He likes red wine too.
Maintenant il a la gueule de bois.	Now he has a hangover.

1b Auxiliary verbs

Some verbs have a use as "auxiliary" verbs. In French, **avoir** (to have) and **être** (to be) are the auxiliary verbs; this means they are used in their various simple tenses, with the past participle of other verbs, in the formation of all the compound tenses. (Compare the use of the verb *to have* in English.)

• avoir:

j'ai mangé	I have eaten
j'avais mangé	I had eaten
j'aurais mangé	I would have eaten

• être:

je suis tombé	I have fallen over
j'étais tombé	I had fallen
je serais tombé	I would have fallen

What verbs govern

All sentences consist of a subject and a predicate. The predicate may be just a verb, or a verb plus more information.

2a Subject + verb + complement

Some verbs just link the subject to the rest of the information, which is known as the "complement." The verb **être** (to be) is frequently used in this way.

Il est pharmacien.	He is a pharmacist.
Elle a été actrice.	She was an actress.

2b Verbs that need no further completion

Le facteur arrive.   The mailman is coming.

In this sentence the verb is complete in itself. Other information could be added, such as **maintenant** (now), or **à vélo** (by bike). The verb would nevertheless be complete. This type of verb is called "intransitive." Verbs which are only intransitive in use are marked "intr" in the Index of this handbook.

2c Verbs that have an object

Il regarde les adresses sur les lettres.   He's looking at the addresses on the letters.

Here, the verb requires a noun phrase (addresses) to complete the sense. The direct object of the verb is the item(s) or person(s) directly affected by the action. **Regarder** is a verb that needs a direct object. Such verbs are called "transitive" and marked "tr" in the Index.

A considerable number of verbs can be either transitive or intransitive. These are marked "tr/intr" (e.g., **changer**).

2d Verb + preposition + object

French verbs do not always have the same relationship with the rest of the sentence as their English counterparts. Verbs that are transitive in English may need a preposition before the object in French; and the converse is true.

Je me suis emparé *de* la bouteille, et j'ai téléphone *au* docteur.	I grabbed the bottle and phoned the doctor.
J'ai attendu le docteur une demi-heure.	I waited half an hour *for* the doctor

A list of verbs like **attendre** would include:

chercher	to look for	**habiter**	to live in/at
demander	to ask for	**regarder**	to look at
écouter	to listen to		

Here it is the English that adds the preposition. When a verb requires a preposition in either language, the preposition is given in the Index. For a full list of these verbs ➤Berlitz *French Grammar Handbook*, 8e.

2e Verbs that have two objects

(i) Direct and indirect objects

Le facteur a donné deux lettres à mon patron.	The postman gave two letters to my boss.

Here the direct object of the verb consists of the two letters, given to the indirect object, the boss.

(ii) Sometimes in English we omit the word "to" in such sentences. In French sentences involving both direct and indirect objects, the indirect object always follows **à**.

Il donne les lettres au patron.	He gives the boss the letters.

When pronouns are involved the word order makes the meaning clear.

Il m'a offert des fleurs.	He gave me some flowers.
Il me les a offertes pour mon anniversaire.	He gave them to me for my birthday.

– Où est ton stylo?	– Where's your pen?
– Je le lui ai donné.	– I gave it to her.

2f   *Reflexive verbs*

(i)   Some verbs express an action that is turned back on the subject: the object is the same person as the subject.

Je me pèse une fois par semaine.	I weigh myself once a week.

(ii)   Sometimes people are doing the action not to themselves but to each other, in which case the subject is invariably plural.

Ils s'aiment à la folie.	They love each other madly.

(iii)   In many cases the French reference to self or each other is not expressed in English.

Je m'habille dans ma chambre.	I get dressed in my room.
Il se fatigue vite.	He gets tired quickly.

(iv)   With some verbs the reflexive idea has largely disappeared, but the grammatical form still applies.

Je me suis aperçu de son indifference.	I noticed his indifference.

2g   *Verbs governing verbs*

(i)   *Combining verbs*

More complex sentences are made in both French and English combining two verbs. The combinations are not always parallel.

J'aime aller en France.	I like to go to France *or* I like going to France.
Je dois partir demain.	I must leave tomorrow.

Je t'invite à m'accompagner.	I invite you to come with me.
J'ai oublié d'acheter des chèques de voyage.	I've forgotten to buy travelers' checks.

Each of these complex sentences in French follows one of two possible patterns:

- verb + infinitive;
- verb + preposition + infinitive.

The infinitive is the part of the verb that has the meaning "to do," "to play" etc. [➤4a].

The commonest prepositions used in the structure are **à** and **de**, and the student needs to check which verb follows which pattern. The Index and larger dictionaries give this information. (➤Berlitz *French Grammar Handbook*, 8f.)

(ii) It should be noted that the French present participle (**jouant**, **cherchant**) cannot be used here, even though in English the form ending in *-ing* may be possible.

J'aime chanter.	I like singing/I like to sing.
Je préfère nager.	I prefer swimming/I prefer to swim.

(A) Some of the verbs followed immediately by an infinitive are the modal verbs [➤3] and:

souhaiter	to wish to
espérer	to hope to
monter	to go up
aller	to go/to be going to
entendre	to hear (someone doing something)
voir	to see (someone doing something)
faire	to have/get something done

Je souhaite vraiment faire sa connaissance.	I really hope to meet him.
On espère vous voir au concert.	We hope to see you at the concert.
Nous allons partir en vacances.	We're going to go on vacation.
On les entend crier.	You can hear them shouting.
Je l'ai vu venir.	I saw him coming.
Je fais réparer la télé.	I'm getting the TV repaired.
Je fais construire une maison.	I'm having a house built.

(B) Verbs requiring **à** before an infinitive include:

apprendre à	to learn to
commencer à	to begin to
demander à	to ask to
hésiter à	to hesitate to
réussir à	to succeed in (doing)
renoncer à	to give up (doing)

J'apprends à faire de la planche à voile.	I'm learning windsurfing.
Il a hésité à parler au patron.	He hesitated to speak to the boss.
On a réussi à réparer le voiture.	We managed to repair the car.

(C) Verbs requiring **de** before an infinitive include:

accuser de	to accuse (*someone of doing*)
demander à (quelqu'un de faire quelque chose)	to ask (*someone to do something*)
essayer de	to try to
oublier de	to forget to
permettre de	to allow to

J'ai oublié d'aller chercher mon appareil.	I forgot to fetch my camera.
Elle m'a accusé de tricher.	She accused me of cheating.
On va essayer de finir avant cinq heures.	We're going to try and finish before five o'clock.

This is a much bigger group than the other two, and most verbs fall into this category.

Attitudes to action: modal verbs

3a   Action of modal verbs

Modal verbs are not usually complete in meaning in themselves: they create a mood for, or an attitude toward, the verb that follows. The following verb must be in the infinitive in French.

Je dois partir.	I must leave.
Pouvez-vous appeler un taxi?	Can you call a taxi?
Je voudrais arriver chez moi avant minuit.	I'd like to get home by midnight.

3b   French modal verbs

devoir	to have to
falloir	to be necessary (only exists in the third-person singular form as an impersonal verb)
pouvoir	to be able to
savoir	to know how to
vouloir	to want to

More examples of their use are given on the corresponding verb pages.

 Devoir, **savoir**, and **vouloir** also have independent uses, as well as modal function. They mean "to owe," "to know" and "to want" respectively.

Verb forms not related to time

4a   *The infinitive*

(i)   This is the name part of the verb, determining its entry in the dictionary and its use as a noun, as a verb in the various structures outlined above, and after certain prepositions.

Infinitives in French can be identified by the endings **-er**, **-ir**, **-re**, and **-oir**. *All infinitives have one of these endings, but the endings are not exclusive to verbs.*

(ii)   *Infinitives as nouns*

le rire	laughter	**le devoir**	duty
le déjeuner	lunch	**le souvenir**	memory, souvenir

Some infinitives appear as nouns, but not all can be used this way; it is advisable to check in a dictionary.

   Sometimes an infinitive may appear as the subject of the verb:

***Travailler* ici me rend malade!**   *Working* here makes me ill!

(iii)   Useful expressions that can be used for any person, in combination with any tense:

pour arriver	in order to arrive	**avant de partir**	before leaving
afin d'arriver	in order to arrive	**sans attendre**	without waiting

4b   *Present participle*

(i)   The present participle can be formed from the **nous** form of the present tense, by replacing the **-ons** with **-ant**.

(ii)   The present participle is used as an adjective and, occasionally, as a noun. It is also used with **en**, meaning "by," "while," "in," "on" doing something; the form does not change, regardless of the associated noun's gender or verb's tense. For example:

Elle est passée nous voir *en rentrant* chez elle.	She popped in to see us on the way home. (*Literally, "while going home"*)

[➤also 4c(iv) below.]

 In French "before doing" and "without doing" both require the *infinitive,* not the present participle: **avant de faire, sans faire.**

 No progressive or continuous present tense can be constructed using this participle.

Je travaille.	I am working.

4c *Past participle*

(i) Past participles of regular verbs are formed by adding **-é** (**-er** erbs, **-i** (**-ir** verbs), or **-u** (**-re** verbs) to the stem of the infinitive. The stem is formed by removing **-er**, **-ir**, or **-re**. Irregular verbs may not follow this pattern, and many past participles need to be learnt individually: e.g., **boire – bu**; **écrire – écrit**; **faire – fait**; **lire – lu**.

(ii) The past participle is used:

* as the second item in all the compound past tenses.
* with any tense of **être** to create the passive form: e.g., **Il a été cassé** (It has been broken);
* as in English as an adjective, when it follows the noun: e.g., **la voiture volée** (the stolen car).

(iii) Note also the French for "after doing something," which uses a past infinitive made with **avoir** or **être** + the past participle.

***Après avoir acheté* les timbres, il est parti.**	*After buying* the stamps, he left.
***Après être arrivés*, ils ont loué une voiture.**	*After arriving*, they hired a car.

(iv) The equivalent of English "having done something," is formed by combining both participles:

| **Ayant acheté les timbres . . .** | Having bought the stamps . . . |

(v)   In literary contexts the past participle of certain verbs – those conjugated with **être** in compound tenses – may be used alone in an absolute construction:

| **Une fois arrivé à Paris, il a cherché un hôtel.** | Having arrived in Paris, he looked for a hotel. |

For rules governing the agreements of the past participle in compound tenses ➤Berlitz *French Grammar Handbook.*

What else do French verbs do?

The various tenses in common use given in the verb tables are listed below, with their characteristic endings and meanings.

For a full study of French tenses ➤Berlitz *French Grammar Handbook*, 11.

5a Pronouns

The verb tables are presented with the personal subject pronouns, which are used in French very much as in English.

- **je** – "I"; (**j'** before vowel or mute **h**).
- **tu** – "you" (singular). This is the form of address for family members, close friends, small children, and pets.
- **il** – "he"; also "it," when the name of a thing is masculine.
- **elle** – "she"; also "it," when the name of a thing is feminine.
- **on** – This is presented in this book as a separate entry because of its great importance in the French language, particularly the spoken language. It is commonly used for "we" (colloquially, alongside **nous**, because the shorter verb forms are quicker), "you" (generally), "they," "everyone," "people," "someone," and occasionally "one."
- **nous** – "we."
- **vous** – "you." Used as the normal form of address to a single individual who is not a close friend or relative and as the plural "you" when talking to a group of people.
- **ils** – "they," Refers to people and things that are either all masculine or a mixture of masculine and feminine.
- **elles** – "they," Refers to people and things that are all feminine.

5b Pronunciation

These few pointers may prove useful when studying verbs.

(i) Pronounciation of pronouns

The **-s**, which is normally silent at the end of pronouns **nous**, **vous**, **ils**, and **elles** must always be pronounced as **z** if the verb begins with a vowel or mute **h**. This is called "*liaison.*"

Ils aiment les films italiens.	They like Italian films.
Nous arrivons à midi.	We are arriving at midday.
Ils habitent à Milan.	They live in Milan.

Note that words beginning with aspirate **h**, marked with an asterisk in the index and in dictionaries, require no liaison.

(ii) *Pronounciation of verb endings*

• **-er**, the ending of very many infinitives, is pronounced like **é**.
• **-ant**, the ending of the present participle, is pronounced without the **-t**, as the single nasal vowel of the word **en**.
• **-e**, **-es**, **-s**, **-x**, **-t** endings on all verbs are silent.
• **-ons**, the ending for **nous** (first-person plural), is pronounced like the end of **bon**, the **-s** being silent.
• **-ez**, the ending for **vous** (second-person plural), is pronounced like **é**.
• **-ent**, the ending for third-person plural verbs, is always silent.
• **-ont** has the same pronunciation as **-ons**.
• **-ais**, **-ait**, **-aient** endings of the imperfect tense are pronounced like "e" in the English word "let."

5c French verb forms given in this book

(i)

Infinitive	➤*4a*
Present participle	➤*4b*
Past participle	➤*4c*

(ii) *Imperative*

(A) Imperatives are given in the verb tables. They are the expressions used for requests and commands. They are normally the **tu**, **nous**, and **vous** present-tense forms *without the subject pronoun*; **-er** verbs drop the final **-s** of the **tu** form except before **y** and **en**.

va-à la maison	go home!	*but:*
vas-y	go to it!	

(B) As the imperative form can sound rather abrupt, it is common to find requests phrased:

Veux-tu/Voulez-vous ouvrir la porte?	Will you open the door?

Or

Tu pourrais/vous pourriez ouvrir la porte?	Could you open the door?

(C) When instructions are given for a process, as in recipes, it is also common to find the infinitive used as the imperative:

Délayer le beurre et le sucre.	Cream the butter and sugar.
Ajouter 500 grammes de farine.	Add 500 grams of flour.

(iii)   *Tenses of the indicative*

The indicative tenses are the ordinary verbs that make statements about what is happening, has happened, or will happen. However, they do not only communicate the timing of the action; they may also give the speaker's or writer's perspective on the event.

Use of tenses in French is not directly equivalent to English. The following examples, taken from the verb **parler** (to speak), make this clear.

(A) Simple tenses (where the verb is a single word)

• Present tense: **je parle**
There are three "regular" patterns for the present tense of verbs whose infinitives end in **-er**, **-ir**, and **-re**. All these and the variants and exceptions are set out in the model verb pages.

The French present tense covers the usages of all three English versions: "I speak," "I am speaking," "I do speak." In journalistic accounts it is also very common to find the present tense used to recount the action of the story more vividly than if a past tense were used. This is called the historic present.

• Imperfect tense: **je parlais**
This tense refers to incomplete or continuing action in the past. It can mean: "I spoke," "I was speaking," "I used to speak" or "I would speak" (often).

With the exception of **être (j'étais)**, all verbs form the imperfect tense using the **nous** form stem from the present tense. Simply remove the **-ons** ending of the present and add the endings:

(je) -ais	**(il/elle/on) -ait**	**(vous) -iez**
(tu) -ais	**(nous) -ions**	**(ils) -aient**

- Simple past: **je parlai**

This tense, used mainly in written narrative to tell the events of the story, means "spoke." In regular verbs the stem is that of the infinitive minus **-er/-ir/-re**. The endings are:

-ai, -as, -a, -âmes, -âtes, -èrent (**-er** verbs)
-is, -is, -it, -îmes, -îtes, -irent (**-ir** and **-re** verbs)

There are a number of irregular verbs, with the endings:

-us, -us, -ut, -ûmes, -ûtes, -urent

(➤ Model French Verb)

- Future: **je parlerai**

The simple future is the equivalent of English "shall speak/will speak." The endings for the future are derived from the present tense of **avoir**:

-ai, -as, -a, -ons, -ez, -ont

These are added to a stem which in most verbs is the whole infinitive (**-er** or **-ir** verbs) or the infinitive minus the final **-e** (**-re** verbs). There are a number of exceptions to this simple rule; these need to be learned individually.

- Conditional: **je parlerais**

This tense means "would speak." The stem is that of the future tense, and the endings are those of the imperfect tense:

-ais, -ais, -ait, -ions, -iez, -aient

(B) Compound tenses (verb consists of two words or more)

- Perfect tense: **j'ai parlé**

This is the tense for completed action in the past, in speech and in writing, meaning "I spoke," "I did speak" or "I have spoken." It is formed from the present tense of **avoir** or **être** and the past participle of the verb. Most verbs use **avoir** as the auxiliary. A small number of very common verbs and *all* reflexive verbs use **être**.

- Past perfect or pluperfect: **j'avais parlé**

This tense means "had spoken." It is formed from the imperfect of **avoir** or **être** and the past participle.

- Past anterior: **j'eus parlé**

This tense is found in written narrative where the main action is conveyed in the simple past. It has the meaning "had spoken." It occurs after conjunctions of time (**quand, dès que, aussitôt que**) and is formed with the simple past of **avoir** or **être** and the past participle.

• Future perfect: **j'aurai parlé**
This tense means "will have spoken." It is formed from the future tense of **avoir** or **être** and the past participle. It expresses probability and must also be used after conjunctions of time (**quand**, **dès que**, **aussitôt que**) referring to the future.

• Conditional perfect: **j'aurais parlé**
The meaning of this tense is "would have spoken." It is formed from the conditional tense of **avoir** or **être** and the past participle.

(iv)   Tenses of the subjunctive

The subjunctive is used in French in subordinate clauses after conjunctions such as **quoique** (although), **pourvu que** (provided that), **afin que** (in order to), and after verbs of wishing, fearing, doubting, and other emotions. It also occurs occasionally as a main verb to express a formalized wish: **Vive la France!**

The present and perfect tenses are the ones most frequently used, and are in practice the main tenses in colloquial use. The imperfect subjunctive may occur occasionally in speech in its shorter forms; this and the pluperfect subjunctive are more likely to be found in literary texts. Giving an English equivalent of each tense is not practical, as often structures do not correspond in the two languages.

• Present tense: **que je parle**
Apart from a few irregular verbs, the present subjunctive is formed from the third-person plural of the present indicative. For the singular and the third person plural, simply delete the **-ent** ending and add the endings:

-e, -es, -e, -ent

The **nous** and **vous** forms are the same as in the imperfect indicative:

-ions, -iez

These endings also apply to irregular verbs, but the stem changes. The verbs that are irregular in the present subjective are:

avoir – que j'aie	que nous *ayons*
être – que je sois	que nous *soyons*
aller – que j'aille	que nous allions
faire – que je fasse	que nous *fassions*
falloir – qu'il faille	
pouvoir – que je puisse	que nous *puissions*
savoir – que je sache	que nous *sachions*
valoir – que je vaille	que nous valions
vouloir – que je veuille	que nous voulions

(The *italics* show **nous** and **vous** forms that are also irregular.)

Je veux que tu *ailles* chez Michel.	I want you to go to Michel's.
Je veux bien lui parler pourvu	I don't mind talking to him
qu'il *vienne* avant dix heures.	provided he comes before ten.

* Perfect tense: **que j'aie parlé**
This is formed from the present subjunctive of **avoir** or **être** plus the past participle.

C'est dommage que tu *aies*	It's a pity *you've lost* your purse.
***perdu* ton porte-monnaie.**	

* Imperfect tense: **que je parlasse**
This tense is not often found except in the third-person singular (**parlât**). It is replaced in conversation by the present subjunctive.

J'ignorais qu'il *possédât* un	I didn't know *he had* a gun . . .
fusil . . .	

* Pluperfect tense: **que j'eusse parlé**
This is formed from the imperfect subjunctive of **avoir** or **être** and the past participle. It is not often found in speech.

. . . et je fus indigné qu'il *eût*	. . . and I was annoyed that *he had*
gardé* un si beau secret.	*kept* such a fine secret to himself.

* (Marcel Pagnol: *La Gloire de mon père*)

(v)   *The passive*

When the action is done *to* the subject of the sentence, the passive form may be needed. This is composed of the appropriate tense of **être** (to be) followed by the past participle.

L'enfant a été blessé.	The child was hurt.

The passive is as widely used in French as it is in English, but sometimes the passive in English is replaced by **on:**

Ici on parle anglais	English is spoken here

Or by a reflexive verb:

Ce vin se trouve facilement en Bourgogne.	That wine is easily found in Burgundy.

5d Asking questions

In French there are three possible ways of asking a question. To ask, "Do you like shellfish," one can say:

• **Aimes-tu les fruits de mer?** (*Verb and subject change places.*)

• **Est-ce que tu aimes les fruits de mer?** (*The formula* **est-ce que** *precedes the statement and makes it into a question.*)

• **Tu aimes les fruits de mer?** (*Same word order as a statement, but the voice tone rises at the end of the sentence, creating the question.*)

The same variations are possible when a question word, such as **quand?** (when?) or **où?** (where?) is involved.

• **Où habitez-vous?**

• **Où est-ce que vous habitez?**

• **Vous habitez où?**

Note that when the subject is a noun phrase, it is only possible to use the first variation by adding a pronoun:

Les Borgia ont-*ils* empoisonné tous leurs ennemis?	Did the Borgias poison all their enemies?

As this is fairly formal, in conversation the second and third forms are more usual for such longer, more complex questions.

5e Not, never, no more

(i) Making statements and questions negative in French involves using one of the following expressions:

ne . . . pas	not
ne . . . plus	no more, no longer
ne . . . rien	nothing, not anything

ne . . . jamais	never, not ever
ne . . . personne	nobody, not anybody
ne . . . que	only, nothing but
ne . . . aucun (+ noun)	no, not any

Je *n'*aime *pas* les fruits de mer.	I don't like sea-food.
Vous *n'*avez *pas* d'allumettes?	Haven't you any matches?
Il *ne* fume *plus.*	He doesn't smoke any more.
Il *ne* boit *rien.*	He doesn't drink anything.
Elle *ne* m'écoute *jamais.*	She never listens to me.
Il *n'*y a *personne.*	There's no one (there).

(ii) These negative expressions are positioned around the verb. In compound tenses the negative expression is usually around the auxiliary verb.

Je *n'*ai *pas* trouvé mon sac.	I haven't found my bag.
Elle *n'*a *rien* bu.	She didn't drink anything.
Nous *n'*y sommes *jamais* allés.	We've never been there.

Except:

On *n'*a vu *personne.*	We didn't see anyone.
Il *n'*a apporté *que* trois bouteilles de vin.	He only bought three bottles of wine.
La police *n'*a trouvé *aucune* trace des voleurs.	The police found no trace of the thieves.

For a more comprehensive treatment ➤Berlitz *French Grammar Handbook.*

B

MODEL FRENCH VERBS

Index of model verbs

Verb tables are set out on the following pages. Some verbs are given in full; others show the full forms of the present, perfect, imperfect, and simple past tenses only, giving the first-person singular of the other tenses. These tenses then follow the patterns laid out in the full conjugation pages.

The following verbs are discussed in detail in Chapters 6 to 10. Notes on similar verbs, usage, and exceptions are appended where appropriate.

6   Full conjugations

6a	**marcher**	to walk
6b	**tomber**	to fall
6c	**se laver**	to wash, get washed
6d	**avoir**	to have
6e	**être**	to be
6f	**être blessé**	to be hurt, wounded

7   -er verbs:

7a	**parler**	to speak
7b	**aller**	to go
7c	**appeler**	to call
7d	**acheter**	to buy
7e	**céder**	to give way
7f	**employer**	to employ
7g	**manger**	to eat
7h	**placer**	to place
7i	**payer**	to pay

8   -ir verbs:

8a	**finir**	to finish
8b	**acquérir**	to acquire
8c	**cueillir**	to pick
8d	**courir**	to run
8e	**dormir**	to sleep
8f	**faillir**	to almost do
8g	**fuir**	to flee
8h	**mourir**	to die

8i	**ouvrir**	to open
8j	**sentir**	to feel
8k	**tenir**	to hold
8l	**vêtir**	to dress

9 -re *verbs:*

9a	**vendre**	to sell
9b	**boire**	to drink
9c	**conclure**	to conclude
9d	**conduire**	to lead, drive
9e	**connaître**	to know
9f	**coudre**	to sew
9g	**croire**	to believe
9h	**dire**	to say
9i	**écrire**	to write
9j	**faire**	to do
9k	**lire**	to read
9l	**mettre**	to put
9m	**moudre**	to grind
9n	**naître**	to be born
9o	**peindre**	to paint
9p	**plaire**	to please
9q	**prendre**	to take
9r	**résoudre**	to resolve
9s	**rire**	to laugh
9t	**soustraire**	to subtract
9u	**suivre**	to follow
9v	**vaincre**	to defeat
9w	**vivre**	to live

10 -oir *verbs:*

10a	**s'asseoir**	to sit down
10b	**devoir**	to have to
10c	**falloir**	to have to
10d	**pleuvoir**	to rain
10e	**pouvoir**	to be able to
10f	**promouvoir**	to promote
10g	**recevoir**	to receive
10h	**savoir**	to know
10i	**valoir**	to be worth
10j	**voir**	to see
10k	**vouloir**	to wish, want

23

Full conjugations

6a Marcher, *to walk*

*Example of verb using **avoir** in compound tenses*

Imperative
marche! (tu)   marchez! (vous)   marchons! (nous)

Present
je marche
tu marches
il/elle marche
on marche
nous marchons
vous marchez
ils/elles marchent

Perfect
j'ai marché
tu as marché
il/elle a marché
on a marché
nous avons marché
vous avez marché
ils/elles ont marché

Imperfect
je marchais
tu marchais
il/elle marchait
on marchait
nous marchions
vous marchiez
ils/elles marchaient

Simple past
je marchai
tu marchas
il/elle marcha
on marcha
nous marchâmes
vous marchâtes
ils/elles marchèrent

Past perfect
j'avais marché
tu avais marché
il/elle avait marché
on avait marché
nous avions marché
vous aviez marché
ils/elles avaient marché

Past anterior
j'eus marché
tu eus marché
il/elle eut marché
on eut marché
nous eûmes marché
vous eûtes marché
ils/elles eurent marché

Present participle	*Past participle*
marchant	marché

Future
je marcherai
tu marcheras
il/elle marchera
on marchera
nous marcherons
vous marcherez
ils/elles marcheront

Future perfect
j'aurai marché
tu auras marché
il/elle aura marché
on aura marché
nous aurons marché
vous aurez marché
ils/elles auront marché

Conditional
je marcherais
tu marcherais
il/elle marcherait
on marcherait
nous marcherions
vous marcheriez
ils/elles marcheraient

Conditional perfect
j'aurais marché
tu aurais marché
il/elle aurait marché
on aurait marché
nous aurions marché
vous auriez marché
ils/elles auraient marché

Present subjunctive
que je marche
que tu marches
qu'il/elle marche
qu'on marche
que nous marchions
que vous marchiez
qu'ils/elles marchent

Perfect subjunctive
que j'aie marché
que tu aies marché
qu'il/elle ait marché
qu'on ait marché
que nous ayons marché
que vous ayez marché
qu'ils/elles aient marché

Imperfect subjunctive
que je marchasse
que tu marchasses
qu'il/elle marchât
qu'on marchât
que nous marchassions
que vous marchassiez
qu'ils/elles marchassent

Pluperfect subjunctive
que j'eusse marché
que tu eusses marché
qu'il/elle eût marché
qu'on eût marché
que nous eussions marché
que vous eussiez marché
qu'ils/elles eussent marché

Notes

1. This example of a verb conjugated with **avoir** in compound tenses is given in full for reference.
2. **Marcher** is a regular **-er** verb; the majority of regular and irregular verbs use **avoir** as the auxiliary verb to form the compound tenses.

J'*ai* bien *travaillé* ce matin.	I'*ve worked* well this morning.
J'*ai gagné* le gros lot!	I'*ve won* the jackpot!
Les copains *ont proposé* d'aller à la plage.	The friends *suggested* going to the beach.
Nous *avons manqué* le train.	We *missed* the train.
Vous *avez retrouvé* votre portefeuille?	*Did* you *find* your wallet?
On *avait fini* de travailler avant midi.	We *had finished* working before midday.
Je *suppose* que tu n'*auras* pas *eu* le temps de lire les documents?	I *suppose* you won't *have had* time to read the documents?
Je suis désolé que vous n'ayez pas pu *assister* à notre mariage.	I'm so sorry you weren't able *to come* to our wedding.
J'*aurais invité* mes parents, mais ils sont en Australie.	I *would have invited* my parents, but they're in Australia.
On *aurait pris* un pot si on *avait eu* le temps.	We *would have had* a drink if we'*d had* time.

6b   Tomber, *to fall*

*Example of verb using **être** in compound tenses*

Present participle	Past participle
tombant	tombé

Imperative

tombe! (tu)   tombez! (vous)   tombons! (nous)

Present
je tombe
tu tombes
il/elle tombe
on tombe
nous tombons
vous tombez
ils/elles tombent

Perfect
je suis tombé/tombée
tu es tombé/tombée
il est tombé
elle est tombée
on est tombé
nous sommes tombés/tombées
vous êtes tombé/tombée/
  tombés/tombées
ils sont tombés
elles sont tombées

Imperfect
je tombais
tu tombais
il/elle tombait
on tombait
nous tombions
vous tombiez
ils/elles tombaient

Simple past
je tombai
tu tombas
il/elle tomba
on tomba
nous tombâmes
vous tombâtes
ils/elles tombèrent

Past perfect
j'étais tombé(-e)
tu étais tombé(-e)
il était tombé
elle était tombée
nous étions tombés(-es)
vous étiez tombé(-e/-s/-es)
ils étaient tombés
elles étaient tombées

Past anterior
je fus tombé(-e)
tu fus tombé(-e)
il fut tombé
elle fut tombée
nous fûmes tombés(-es)
vous fûtes tombé(-e/-s/-es)
ils furent tombés
elles furent tombées

Future
je tomberai
tu tomberas
il/elle tombera
on tombera
nous tomberons
vous tomberez
ils/elles tomberont

Future perfect
je serai tombé(-e)
tu seras tombé(-e)
il sera tombé on sera tombé
elle sera tombée
nous serons tombés(-es)
vous serez tombé(-e/-s/-es)
ils seront tombés
elles seront tombées

Conditional
je tomberais
tu tomberais
il/elle tomberait
on tomberait
nous tomberions
vous tomberiez
ils/elles tomberaient

Conditional perfect
je serais tombé(-e)
tu serais tombé(-e)
il serait tombé
elle serait tombée
on serait tombé
nous serions tombés(-es)
vous seriez tombé(-e/-s/-es)
ils seraient tombés
elles seraient tombées

Present subjunctive
que je tombe
que tu tombes
qu'il/elle tombe
qu'on tombe
que nous tombions
que vous tombiez
qu'ils/elles tombent

Perfect subjunctive
que je sois tombé(-e)
que tu sois tombé(-e)
qu'il soit tombé
qu'elle soit tombée
qu'on soit tombé
que nous soyons tombés(-es)
que vous soyez tombé(-e/-s/-es)
qu'ils soient tombés
qu'elles soient tombées

Imperfect subjunctive
que je tombasse
que tu tombasses
qu'il/elle tombât
qu'on tombât
que nous tombassions
que vous tombassiez
qu'ils/elles tombassent

Pluperfect subjunctive
que je fusse tombé(-e)
que tu fusses tombé(-e)
qu'il fût tombé
qu'elle fût tombé
qu'on fût tombé
que nous fussions tombés(-es)
que vous fussiez tombé(-e/-s/-es)
qu'ils fussent tombés
qu'elles fussent tombées

Notes

1. The verbs that are conjugated with **être** in compound tenses are listed under the auxiliary verb itself (**➤être** *5*).

2. All compound tenses using auxiliary **être** require gender agreements on the past participle. The agreement is with the subject of the verb, and may be feminine singular (add an **-e**), masculine plural (add an **-s**), or feminine plural (add **-es**). All possible variations are given in these verb tables. The full list of possible alternatives is given here for the perfect tense; abbreviated forms are given in subsequent compound tenses.

3. A plural agreement is possible for **on est tombés**, where meaning clearly requires it.

4. **Tomber** is a regular **-er** verb.

Je *suis tombé* dans la rue.	I *fell over* in the street.
Sans la ceinture de sécurité, il *serait tombé* à l'eau.	Without the safety belt, *he would have fallen* in the water.
Elle *est tombée* amoureuse.	She'*s fallen* in love.
On m'a dit qu'il *était tombé* d'une fenêtre.	They told me he'*d fallen* out of a window.
On *est allés* à Versailles.	We *went* to Versailles.
Les enfant *sont sortis* à cinq heures.	The children *went out* at five o'clock.
Le train *est arrivé* à l'heure.	The train *arrived* on time.
Mon poisson rouge *est mort*.	My goldfish *has died*.
Vous *étiez parti* avant mon arrivée.	You *had left* before I arrived.
On *était* tous *retournés* chez lui.	We *had* all *gone back* to his place.
Je *serais parti* sans lui . . .	I *would have left* without him . . .
– Où est Patrick?	– Where's Patrick?
– Il *sera parti* pour Rome.	– He'*ll have set off* for Rome.

6c   Se laver, *to wash (oneself)*
Reflexive -er verb

Present participle	**Past participle**
me lavant /te lavant /se lavant /	lavé
nous lavant /vous lavant	

Imperative

lave-toi! (tu)	lavez-vous! (vous)	lavons-nous! (nous)

Present	**Perfect**
je me lave	je me suis lavé/lavée
tu te lave	tu t'es lavé/lavée
il/elle se lave	il s'est lavé
on se lave	elle s'est lavée
nous nous lavons	on s'est lavé
vous vous lavez	nous nous sommes lavés/lavées
ils/elles se lavent	vous vous êtes lavé/lavée/
	lavés/lavées
	ils se sont lavés
	elles se sont lavées

Imperfect	**Simple past**
je me lavais	je me lavai
tu te lavais	tu te lavas
il/elle se lavait	il/elle se lava
on se lavait	on se lava
nous nous lavions	nous nous lavâmes
vous vous laviez	vous vous lavâtes
ils/elles se lavaient	ils/elles se lavèrent

Past perfect	**Past anterior**
je m'étais lavé(-e)	je me fus lavé(-e)
tu t'étais lavé(-e)	tu te fus lavé(-e)
il s'était lavé	il se fut lavé
elle s'était lavée	elle se fut lavée
on s'était lavé	on se fut lavé
nous nous étions lavés(-es)	nous nous fûmes lavés(-es)
vous vous étiez lavé(-e/-s/-es)	vous vous fûtes lavé(-e/-s/-es)
ils se sont lavés	ils se furent lavés
elles se sont lavées	elles se furent lavées

Future
je me laverai
tu te laveras
il/elle se lavera
on se lavera
nous nous laverons
vous vous laverez
ils/elles se laveront

Conditional
je me laverais
tu te laverais
il/elle se laverait
on se laverait
nous nous laverions
vous vous laveriez
ils/elles se laveraient

Present subjunctive
que je me lave
que tu te laves
qu'il/elle se lave
qu'on se lave
que nous nous lavions
que vous vous laviez
qu'ils/elles se lavent

Imperfect subjunctive
que je me lavasse
que tu te lavasses
qu'il/elle se lavât
qu'on se lavât
que nous nous lavassions
que vous vous lavassiez
qu'ils/elles se lavassent

Future perfect
je me serai lavé(-e)
tu te seras lavé(-e)
il se sera lavé
elle se sera lavée
on se sera lavé
nous nous serons lavés(-es)
vous vous serez lavé(-e/-s/-es)
ils se seront lavés
elles se seront lavées

Conditional perfect
je me serais lavé(-e)
tu te serais lavé(-e)
il se serait lavé
elle se serait lavée
on se serait lavé
nous nous serions lavés(-es)
vous vous seriez lavé(-e/-s/-es)
ils se seraient lavés
elles se seraient lavées

Perfect subjunctive
que je me sois lavé(-e)
que tu te sois lavé(-e)
qu'il se soit lavé
qu'elle se soit lavée
qu'on se soit lavé
que nous nous soyons lavés(-es)
que vous vous soyez lavé(-e/-s/-es)
qu'ils se soient lavés
qu'elles se soient lavées

Pluperfect subjunctive
que je me fusse lavé (-e)
que te fusses lavé(-e)
qu'il se fût lavé
qu'elle se fût lavée
qu'on se fût lavé
que nous nous fussions lavés (-es)
que vous fussiez lavé(-e/-s/-es)
qu'ils se fussent lavés
qu'elles se fussent lavées

Notes

1. All reflexive verbs in French use **être** in compound tenses, and the rules for agreement of the past participle apply as with nonreflexive verbs using **être**, *where the reflexive pronoun is the direct object of the verb.* (In verbs where the reflexive pronoun is the indirect object, there is no agreement of the past particple.)

2. Full alternatives according to gender (masculine or feminine) and number (singular or plural) are given for the perfect tense; in the other compound tenses the alternatives are given in abbreviated form.

3. It is possible to make masculine or feminine plural agreement for **on s'est lavés/-es**, where the sense is clearly plural.

Le matin	**In the morning**
Je *me réveille* normalement vers sept heures. Je *me lève* vite. J'écoute le bulletin météo en *me rasant.* Puis *je me brosse* les dents et je *me lave* la figure avant de *m'habiller.*	I normally *wake up* around seven. I *get up* quickly. I listen to the weather report while *shaving.* Then I *brush* my teeth and *wash* my face before *getting dressed.*
Elle *s'est réveillée* vers sept heures.	She *woke up* around seven o'clock.
Elle *s'est demande* pourquoi le chien hurlait.	She *wondered* why the dog was howling.
Je *m'entends* bien avec mes parents.	I *get on* well with my parents.
Je *m'entendais* bien avec ma grand'mère.	I *used to get on* well with my grandmother.
Les jeunes *se sont* bien *amusés* en Italie.	The young people *enjoyed themselves* in Italy.
Sans lui, on *se serait* bien *amusés.*	Without him, we *would have enjoyed* ourselves.
Installez-vous ici, près de la fenêtre.	*Sit here*, near the window.
Les ouvriers *s'étaient mis* à réparer le toit.	The workmen *had started* repairing the roof.
Recueillez-vous un instant avant de quitter cette cathédrale.	*Meditate* a moment before leaving this cathedral.

6d Avoir, *to have*
Auxiliary verb

Present participle	**Past participle**
ayant	eu

Imperative
aie! (tu)   ayez! (vous)   ayons! (nous)

Present	**Perfect**
j'ai	j'ai eu
tu as	tu as eu
il/elle a	il/elle a eu
on a	on a eu
nous avons	nous avons eu
vous avez	vous avez eu
ils/elles ont	ils ont eu

Imperfect	**Simple past**
j'avais	j'eus
tu avais	tu eus
il/elle avait	il/elle eut
on avait	on eut
nous avions	nous eûmes
vous aviez	vous eûtes
ils/elles avaient	ils/elles eurent

Past perfect	**Past anterior**
j'avais eu	j'eus eu
tu avais eu	tu eus eu
il/elle avait eu	il/elle eut eu
on avait eu	on eut eu
nous avions eu	nous eûmes eu
vous aviez eu	vous eûtes eu
ils/elles avaient eu	ils/elles eurent eu

Future	**Future perfect**
j'aurai	j'aurai eu
tu auras	tu auras eu
il/elle aura	il/elle aura eu
on aura	on aura eu
nous aurons	nous aurons eu
vous aurez	vous aurez eu
ils/elles auront	ils/elles auront eu

Conditional
j'aurais
tu aurais
il/elle aurait
on aurait
nous aurions
vous auriez
ils/elles auraient

Conditional perfect
j'aurais eu
tu aurais eu
il/elle aurait eu
on aurait eu
nous aurions eu
vous auriez eu
ils/elles auraient eu

Present subjunctive
que j'aie
que tu aies
qu'il/elle ait
qu'on ait
que nous ayons
que vous ayez
qu'ils/elles aient

Perfect subjunctive
que j'aie eu
que tu aies eu
qu'il/elle ait eu
qu'on ait eu
que nous ayons eu
que vous ayez eu
qu'ils/elles aient eu

Imperfect subjunctive
que j'eusse
que tu eusses
qu'il/elle eût
qu'on eût
que nous eussions
que vous eussiez
qu'ils/elles eussent

Pluperfect subjunctive
que j'eusse eu
que tu eusses
qu'il/elle eût eu
qu'on eût eu
que nous eussions eu
que vous eussiez eu
qu'ils/elles eussent eu

Notes

1. **Avoir** is used as the auxiliary verb for the majority of verbs in compound tenses.
2. Note the impersonal phrase **il y a**, meaning "there is" and "there are" used in all common tenses. **Il y a** also means "ago," and in this use is invariable.
3. Note also the idiomatic expressins using **avoir: avoir faim** (to be hungry), **avoir chaud** (to be hot), etc. [➤ Verb index.]

J'*ai* dix-sept ans.	I'*m* seventeen.
Chez moi j'*ai* une machine à laver et un lave-vaisselle.	At home I *have* a washing machine and a dishwasher.

J'*ai* deux frères.	I *have* two brothers.
Quand j'étais petite, j'*avais* une belle poupée.	When I was little, I *had* a lovely doll.
En ville il y *a* deux cinémas.	There *are* two movie houses in town.
Il y *a* deux ans, je suis allé visiter le Louvre.	I went to visit the Louvre two years ago.
Il y *a eu* un accident.	There's *been* an accident.
Combien d'étudiants y *aurait*-il?	How many students *would* there *be*?
Nous *avons* besoin de votre aide.	We need your help.
J'*ai* sommeil.	I'm sleepy.
J'*ai eu* de la chance.	I've been lucky (I've *had* some luck).
Elle *aura* une soixantaine d'années.	She'll *be* about sixty.
J'*avais* peur du chien des voisins.	I *was* afraid of the neighbors' dog.
Le train partit sans qu'il *eût* le temps de lui dire au revoir.	The train left without his *having* time to say good-bye to her.

Examples of auxiliary use

Je n'*ai* pas encore acheté de magnétoscope.	I *have*n't yet bought a video recorder.
Je n'*aurais* jamais pensé à cela.	I *would* never *have* thought of that.
Il n'*avait* pas préparé son discours.	He *had*n't prepared his speech.
Dès qu'il *eut* vu la fille, il partit.	As soon as he *had* seen the girl, he left.
Je regrette qu'il ne t'*ait* pas invité.	I'm sorry he *did*n't invite you.
Ce journaliste n'*aurait* pas écrit ça!	That journalist *would* not *have* written that!
Il *aura* fallu des années pour tout remettre en ordre.	It *will have* taken years to put everything straight.

6e Etre, *to be*

Auxiliary verb used in some compound tenses and for the passive

---

Imperative

sois! (tu)   soyez! (vous)   soyons! (nous)

Present

je suis
tu es
il/elle est
on est
nous sommes
vous êtes
ils/elles sont

Perfect

j'ai été
tu as été
il/elle a été
on a été
nous avons été
vous avez été
ils/elles ont été

Imperfect

j'étais
tu étais
il/elle était
on était
nous étions
vous étiez
ils/elles étaient

Simple past

je fus
tu fus
il/elle fut
on fut
nous fûmes
vous fûtes
ils/elles furent

Past perfect

j'avais été
tu avais été
il/elle avait été
on avait été
nous avions été
vous aviez été
ils/elles avaient été

Past anterior

j'eus été
tu eus été
il/elle eut été
on eut été
nous eûmes été
vous eûtes été
ils/elles eurent été

Present participle	**Past perfect**
étant	été

Future	**Future perfect**
je serai	j'aurai été
tu seras	tu auras été
il/elle sera	il/elle aura été
on sera	on aura été
nous serons	nous aurons été
vous serez	vous aurez été
ils/elles seront	ils/elles auront été

Conditional	**Conditional perfect**
je serais	j'aurais été
tu serais	tu aurais été
il/elle serait	il/elle aurait été
on serait	on aurait été
nous serions	nous aurions été
vous seriez	vous auriez été
ils/elles seraient	ils/elles auraient été

Present subjunctive	**Perfect subjunctive**
que je sois	que j'aie été
que tu sois	que tu aies été
qu'il/elle soit	qu'il/elle ait été
qu'on soit	qu'on ait été
que nous soyons	que nous ayons été
que vous soyez	que vous ayez été
qu'ils/elles soient	qu'ils/elles aient été

Imperfect subjunctive	**Pluperfect subjunctive**
que je fusse	que j'eusse été
que tu fusses	que tu eusses été
qu'il/elle fût	qu'il/elle eût été
qu'on fût	qu'on eût été
que nous fussions	que nous eussions été
que vous fussiez	que vous eussiez été
qu'ils/elles fussent	qu'ils/elles eussent été

Notes

1. **être** is used as the auxiliary verb in compound tenses for all reflexive verbs, as well as the following thirteen intransitive verbs of motion, and their compounds:

aller	venir
partir	arriver
monter	descendre
sortir	entrer
mourir	naître
rester	retourner
tomber	

These form six pairs of verbs denoting movement in opposite directions, plus **tomber.**

2. Note that the auxiliary uses of **être** are in the formation of compound tenses, and in the passive voice [➤4c (ii), 5c (v)].

3. There is no French equivalent for the English progressive continuous present form, as in "I am writing." For this, either the simple present tense is used, or the expression **être en train de faire**, if the continuity is to be stressed.

Examples of use as linking verb

Je *suis* de nationalité britannique.	I *am* British.
Il *est* ingénieur.	He's an engineer.
Nous *sommes* très déçus.	We're very disappointed.
Les livres *sont* dans le sac.	The books *are* in the bag.
Quand j'*étais* petite, j'*étais* très timide.	When I *was* little, I *was* very shy.
Il *est* cinq heures.	It's five o'clock.
On *sera* à Paris le 20 octobre.	We'*ll be* in Paris on the 20th of October.
Les chants d'oiseaux *seront* bientôt remplacés par des bruits mécaniques.	Birdsong *will* soon *be* replaced by the noise of machinery.
Je *serais* très contente de partir.	I *should be* very pleased to leave.
Elle a dit qu'elle *aurait été* très contente de partir.	She said she *would have been* very pleased to leave.

Examples of auxiliary use

Je *suis* arrivé avant toi.	I arrived before you.
Ils *étaient* partis à huit heures.	They had left at eight.
Je me *suis* levé avant six heures.	I got up before six.
Il ne *serait* pas parti sans les autres.	He wouldn't have left without the others.
Bien que je *sois* tombé de l'échelle, je ne me *suis* pas fait mal.	Although I fell off the ladder, I didn't hurt myself.
Nous *sommes* arrivés à un point critique.	We've reached a critical point.
Il croyait qu'on *était* arrivés à un point critique.	He thought we'd reached a critical point.
On se *serait* déjà arrêtés, si le patron n'*était* pas arrivé!	We would have stopped already if the boss hadn't arrived!
Ces tarifs ont *été* négociés avec chaque chaîne.	These rates have been negotiated with each TV channel.

6f   Etre blessé, *to be hurt*
*Full conjugation of the passive using the verb **être***

Imperative

sois . . . (tu)   soyez . . . (vous)   soyons . . . (nous)

Present
je suis blessé(-e)
tu es blessé(-e)
il est blessé
elle est blessée
on est blessé
nous sommes blessés(-es)
vous êtes blessé(-e/-s/-es)
ils sont blessés
elles sont blessées

Perfect
j'ai été blessé(-e)
tu as été blessé(-e)
il a été blessé
elle a été blessée
on a été blessé
nous avons été blessés(-es)
vous avez été blessé(-e/-s/-es)
ils ont été blessés
elles ont été blessées

Imperfect
j'étais blessé(-e)
tu étais blessé(-e)
il était blessé
elle était blessée
on était blessé
nous étions blessés(-es)
vous étiez blessé(-e/-s/-es)
ils étaient blessés
elles étaient blessées

Simple past
je fus blessé(-e)
tu fus blessé(-e)
il fut blessé
elle fut blessée
on fut blessé
nous fûmes blessés(-es)
vous fûtes blessé(-e/-s/-es)
ils furent blessés
elles furent blessées

Notes

1. The verb forms presented on other pages are all in the ordinary form, known as the "active voice." The "passive voice," or "passive" [➤5c (v)] is used when the verb's action is done to the subject by another agent, known or implied.
2. It is formed in French as in English by using the full range of tenses of the verb **êt**re (to be) [➤**être**] and the past participle. Any transitive verb can be used passively.
3. Note again differences between the two languages where verbs do not have the same patterns of use in French as in English. A passive construction is impossible with verbs such as **donner** because, in the active voice, the person receiving is not a direct object, but an indirect object.
Donner un cadeau à quelqu'un.   Give a present to someone.
Téléphoner à quelqu'un.   Telephone someone.
4. The imperative can be found occasionally.
Sois béni!   Bless you!

Present participle	**Past participle**
étant blessé(-e/-s/-es)	été blessé(-e/-s/-es)

Past perfect	**Past anterior**
j'avais été blessé(-e)	j'eus été blessé(-e)

Future	**Future perfect**
je serai blessé(-e)	j'aurai été blessé(-e)

Conditional	**Conditional perfect**
je serais blessé(-e)	j'aurais été blessé(-e)

Present subjunctive	**Perfect subjunctive**
que je sois blessé(-e)	que j'aie été blessé(-e)

Imperfect subjunctive	**Pluperfect subjunctive**
que je fusse blessé(-e)	que j'eusse été blessé(-e)

Je *suis aimé.*	I *am loved.*
Toutes les places *ont été prises*	All the seats *have been taken.*
Je regrette que la maison *soit vendue.*	I'm sorry the house *is sold.*
J'ai peur qu'il *ait été blessé.*	I'm afraid he's *been injured.*
Le livre a *été retrouvé* mais il *était abîmé.*	The book *was found* but it *was ruined.*
Les fleurs *ont été données.*	The flowers *were given.*
On m'a donné les fleurs.	I was given the flowers.
On m'a téléphoné.	I was telephoned.

-er verbs

7a Parler, *to speak*
Regular -er verb

Imperative
parle! (tu)   parlez! (vous)   parlons! (nous)

Present
je parle
tu parles
il/elle parle
on parle
nous parlons
vous parlez
ils/elles parlent

Perfect
j'ai parlé
tu as parlé
il/elle a parlé
on a parlé
nous avons parlé
vous avez parlé
ils/elles ont parlé

Imperfect
je parlais
tu parlais
il/elle parlait
on parlait
nous parlions
vous parliez
ils/elles parlaient

Simple past
je parlai
tu parlas
il/elle parla
on parla
nous parlâmes
vous parlâtes
ils/elles parlèrent

Similar verbs

aimer	like	**jurer**	swear
briser	break	**louer**	hire, rent
chercher	look for	**montrer**	show
demander	ask	**oublier**	forget
écouter	listen (to)	**présenter**	present
fermer	shut	**trouver**	find
gronder	scold	**vérifier**	check
hésiter	hesitate	**verser**	pour
inviter	invite		

Notes

1. This is the pattern for the regular **-er** verb conjugation (➤also full conjugation of **marcher**, 6a).

2. This is by far the largest group of verbs and is the conjugation into which newly created verbs are added.

3. On the following pages are conjugations of -er verbs that have slight spelling modifications in certain forms.

4. -ier verbs follow the pattern above, which produces forms with -ii- in the imperfect indicative and present subjunctive:
Nous appréciions; vous appréciiez.

Present participle	**Past participle**
parlant	parlé

Past perfect	**Past anterior**
j'avais parlé	j'eus parlé

Future	**Future perfect**
je parlerai	j'aurai parlé

Conditional	**Conditional perfect**
je parlerais	j'aurais parlé

Present subjunctive	**Perfect subjunctive**
que je parle	que j'ai parlé

Imperfect subjunctive	**Pluperfect subjunctive**
que je parlasse	que j'eusse parlé

Conversation à sept heures du matin	*A conversation at seven o'clock in the morning*
– Qu'est-ce que tu *cherches?*	– What are you *looking for?*
– Je *cherche* mon stylo. Je l'*ai laissé* sur la table.	– I'm *looking for* my pen. I *left* it on the table.
– Alors *regarde* sous la table!	– Then look under the table.
– J'y *ai* déjà *regardé.*	– I've already *looked* there.
– Eh bien, tu *demanderas* à ta soeur! Elle te *prêtera* un stylo.	– Well, you *must ask* your sister. She'll *lend* you a pen.
– Impossible! elle est encore fâchée parce que j'ai abîmé le stylo qu'elle a *acheté* hier matin. Pendant que j'*étudiais* ces lettres, elle *comptait* ses crayons et ses stylos!	– Impossible. She's still angry because I ruined the pen she *bought* yesterday. While I *was studying* those letters, she *was counting* her pens and pencils.
– Si tu ne *trouves* pas ton stylo à toi, tu vas en *acheter* un autre tout de suite!	– If you don't *find* your pen, you're going *to buy* another straight away.

7b   Aller, *to go*

Irregular -er verb

Imperative

va! (tu)   allez! (vous)   allons! (nous)

Present
je vais
tu vas
il/elle va
on va
nous allons
vous allez
ils/elles vont

Perfect
je suis allé/allée
tu es allé/allée
il est allé
elle est allée
on est allé
nous sommes allés/allées
vous êtes allé/allée/allés/allées
ils sont allés
elles sont allées

Imperfect
j'allais
tu allais
il/elle allait
on allait
nous allions
vous alliez
ils/elles allaient

Simple past
j'allai
tu allas
il/elle alla
on alla
nous allâmes
vous allâtes
ils/elles allèrent

Notes

1. **Aller** is the only verb of its type, and is the only irregular **-er** verb.
2. It is used with the infinitive as an immediate future tense, like English: e.g., je vais faire . . ., "I am going to do . . ." This form is extremely common in speech.

Examples of use as a full verb

– **Où *vas*-tu?**
– **Je *vais* au cinéma.**
– **Moi, j'y *suis allée* hier.**
– **On y *serait allés* à Noël.**

– Where are you going?
– I'm going to the movies/cinema.
– I went there yesterday myself.
– We would have gone there at Christmas.

Present participle	*Past participle*
allant	allé

Past perfect	*Past anterior*
j'étais allé(-e)	je fus allé(-e)

Future	*Future perfect*
j'irai	je serai allé(-e)

Conditional	*Conditional perfect*
j'irais	je serais allé(-e)

Present subjunctive	*Perfect subjunctive*
que j'aille	que je sois allé(-e)

Imperfect subjunctive	*Pluperfect subjunctive*
que j'allasse	que je fusse allé(-e)

Examples of use with an infinitive to express the immediate future

Qu'est-ce qu'on *va faire* demain?	What *are* we *going to do* tomorrow?
On *va passer* la matinée au musée.	We're *going to spend* the morning at the museum.
Ils *vont arriver* à midi.	They're *going to arrive* at noon.
On *allait passer* l'après-midi à la plage, mais il a plu.	We were *going to spend* the afternoon at the beach, but it rained.

7c Appeler, *to call*

*Regular **-er** verb; consonant doubles before mute ending and in future and conditional tenses*

Imperative

appelle! (tu)   appelez! (vous)   appelons! (nous)

Present	**Perfect**
j'appelle	j'ai appelé
tu appelles	tu as appelé
il/elle appelle	il/elle a appelé
on appelle	on a appelé
nous appelons	nous avons appelé
vous appelez	vous avez appelé
ils/elles appellent	ils ont appelé

Imperfect	**Simple past**
j'appelais	j'appelai
tu appelais	tu appelas
il/elle appelait	il/elle appela
on appelait	on appela
nous appelions	nous appelâmes
vous appeliez	vous appelâtes
ils/elles appelaient	ils/elles appelèrent

Similar verbs

rappeler	remind	**rejeter**	reject
se rappeler	remember	**projeter**	project
jeter	throw	**ruisseler**	flow

Notes

The majority of verbs in **-eler** and **-eter** are spelled this way. The doubling of the letter **-l-** or **-t-** occurs when the vowel **-e-** is an open sound, as in English "let"; that is, when the following ending is not pronounced, and also throughout the future tense. (➤**acheter**, 7d, for those using **è** instead of **-tt-**, **-ll-**.)

Present participle	**Past participle**
appelant	appelé

Past perfect	**Past anterior**
j'avais appelé	j'eus appelé
Future	**Future perfect**
j'appellerai	j'aurai appelé
Conditional	**Conditional perfect**
j'appellerais	j'aurais appelé
Present subjunctive	**Perfect subjunctive**
que j'appelle	que j'aie appelé
Imperfect subjunctive	**Pluperfect subjunctive**
que j'appelasse	que j'eusse appelé

– Je m'*appelle* Marcel.
Comment vous *appelez*-vous?

– I'm *called* Marcel.
What's your name?

Je l'ai *appelée* hier soir.

I *called* her yesterday evening.

**Je crois qu'on *rejettera*
ma suggestion.**

I think they'*ll reject* my
suggestion.

**"*Rappelle*-toi, Barbara,
Il pleuvait sans cesse sur
Brest ce jour-là . . ."**
Paroles (Jacques Prévert)

"*Do you remember,* Barbara,
It was raining endlessly
on Brest that day . . ."

7d   Acheter, *to buy*

Regular -er verb requiring -è- before mute ending and in future and conditional tenses

---

Imperative
achète! (tu)   achetez! (vous)   achetons! (nous)

Present	**Perfect**
j'achète	j'ai acheté
tu achètes	tu as acheté
il/elle achète	il/elle a acheté
on achète	on a acheté
nous achetons	nous avons acheté
vous achetez	vous avez acheté
ils/elles achètent	ils/elles ont acheté

Imperfect	**Simple past**
j'achetais	j'achetai
tu achetais	tu achetas
il/elle achetait	il/elle acheta
on achetait	on acheta
nous achetions	nous achetâmes
vous achetiez	vous achetâtes
ils/elles achetaient	ils/elles achetèrent

Similar verbs

celer	conceal	**marteler**	hammer
ciseler	chisel	**mener**	lead
congeler	freeze	**modeler**	model
déceler	detect	**peler**	peel
dégeler	thaw	**peser**	weigh
geler	freeze	**racheter**	buy back
haleter	pant	**semer**	sow
lever	lift	**surgeler**	deep-freeze

Notes

1. Compounds of the verbs also follow the spelling pattern of **acheter; peler; mener; peser; lever;** and **semer.**

Present participle	Past participle
achetant	acheté

Past perfect	Past anterior
j'avais acheté	j'eus acheté

Future
j'achèterai

Future perfect
j'aurai acheté

Conditional
j'achèterais

Conditional perfect
j'aurais acheté

Present subjunctive
que j'achète

Perfect subjunctive
que j'aie acheté

Imperfect subjunctive
que j'achetasse

Pluperfect subjunctive
que j'eusse acheté

Je me *lève* vers sept heures.

I *get up* around seven.

Je *sème* à tout vent.
(Motto of Larousse publishing house.)

I *sow* in all directions.

Tu nous *mènes* où?

Where *are* you *leading* us?

Au supermarché

At the supermarket

– Bonjour, madame. Excusez-moi. J'*ai acheté* ce paquet de petits pois *congelés* hier, mais je les *ai pesés* chez moi et ils ne *pèsent* pas 200 grammes.

– Hello, ma'am. Excuse me. I *bought* this packet of *frozen* peas yesterday, but I *weighed* them at home and they *don't weigh* 200g.

– Désolée, monsieur. Quand j'*aurai pelé* ces pommes de terre, je *me lèverai* pour vous chercher un autre paquet.

– Terribly sorry, sir. When I've *peeled* these potatoes, I'll *get up* and find you another pack.

49

7e   Céder, to give way, cede
Regular -er verb changing -é- to -è-

Imperative
cède! (tu)   cédez! (vous)   cédons! (nous)

Present	Perfect
je cède	j'ai cédé
tu cèdes	tu as cédé
il/elle cède	il/elle a cédé
on cède	on a cédé
nous cédons	nous avons cédé
vous cédez	vous avez cédé
ils/elles cèdent	ils ont cédé

Imperfect	Simple past
je cédais	je cédai
tu cédais	tu cédas
il/elle cédait	il/elle céda
on cédait	on céda
nous cédions	nous cédâmes
vous cédiez	vous cédâtes
ils/elles cédaient	ils/elles cédèrent

Similar verbs

accélérer	speed up	**intégrer**	include
adhérer	adhere	**interpréter**	interpret
célébrer	celebrate	**précéder**	precede
déléguer	delegate	**régler**	settle
espérer	hope	**succéder**	succeed

Notes

1. Any verb having **-é-** before the last syllable of the infinitive follows this pattern. There are many combinations: **-ébrer; -écer; -écher; -éder; -égler; -égner; -égrer; -éguer; -éler; -émer; -éner; -éper; -équer; -érer; -éser; -éter; -étrer; -évrer; -éyer.**
2. The **-è-** occurs in the present tenses, when the ending is not heard, and in the singular imperative.

Répétez après moi . . .	*Repeat after me . . .*
Je ne veux pas que tu répètes ça aux autres!	I don't want you *to repeat* that to the others!

Present participle	**Past participle**
cédant	cédé

Past perfect	**Past anterior**
j'avais cédé	j'eus cédé
Future	**Future perfect**
je céderai	j'aurai cédé
Conditional	**Conditional perfect**
je céderais	j'aurais cédé
Present subjunctive	**Perfect subjunctive**
que je cède	que j'aie cédé
Imperfect subjunctive	**Pluperfect subjunctive**
que je cédasse	que j'eusse cédé

Vous n'*avez* pas *complété* le travail.	You *haven't finished* the work.
J'*espérais* te voir au bureau.	I *was hoping* to see you at the office.
Il *a abrégé* son voyage.	He *cut short* his journey.
J'*interpréterai* ce vers de poésie d'après le contexte.	I *shall interpret* this line of poetry according to the context.
L'anniversaire	*The birthday*
– J'*espère* que tu *célébreras* tes vingt ans en nous invitant tous au resto!	– I *hope* you *will celebrate* your twentieth birthday by inviting us all to eat out!
– Bien sûr, mais je te *délègue* la responsabilité de réserver la table!	– Of course, but I'*m delegating* you to reserve the table.
– Ah bon! Et je suppose que je dois *régler* l'addition après!	– Oh right! And I suppose I have to *pay* the bill after!

7f   Employer, *to work, employ*
Regular -er verb ending in -oyer or -uyer

Imperative
emploie! (tu)   employez! (vous)   employons! (nous)

Present	Perfect
j'emploie	j'ai employé
tu emploies	tu as employé
il/elle emploie	il/elle a employé
on emploie	on a employé
nous employons	nous avons employé
vous employez	vous avez employé
ils/elles emploient	ils/elles ont employé

Imperfect	Simple past
j'employais	j'employai
tu employais	tu employas
il/elle employait	il/elle employa
on employait	on employa
nous employions	nous employâmes
vous employiez	vous employâtes
ils/elles employaient	ils/elles employèrent

Similar verbs

appuyer	lean; press	**noyer**	drown
broyer	grind	**ployer**	bend; sag
ennuyer	bore	**tutoyer**	address someone as "tu"
essuyer	wipe	**vouvoyer**	address someone as "vous"

Notes

1. Verbs in **-oyer** and **-uyer** follow this pattern.
2. **Envoyer** and **renvoyer** differ in the future and conditional tenses with irregular forms: **j'enverrai/je renverrai**, "I will send/resend."

Present participle	*Past participle*
employant	employé

Past perfect	*Past anterior*
j'avais employé	j'eus employé

Future	*Future perfect*
j'employerai	j'aurai employé

Conditional	*Conditional perfect*
j'employerais	j'aurais employé

Present subjunctive	*Perfect subjunctive*
employe	que j'aie employé

Imperfect subjunctive	*Pluperfect subjunctive*
que j'employasse	que j'eusse employé

J'*enverrai* ce paquet à ma soeur la semaine prochaine.	I *shall send* this package to my sister next week.
On peut se *tutoyer* maintenant.	We can *call* each other *"tu"* now.
As-tu bien *essuyé* les verres?	*Have* you *dried* the glasses properly?
Elle m'*envoie* le journal régional tous les samedis.	She *sends* me the local paper every Saturday.
Délayez bien la farine dans le lait.	*Mix* the flour well into the milk.
On fait très peu pour *enrayer* le chômage.	They're not doing much *to curb* unemployment.

7g　Manger, *to eat*
Regular -er verb ending in -ger

Imperative

mange! (tu)　　　　mangez! (vous)　　　　*mangeons!* (nous)

Present
je mange
tu manges
il/elle mange
on mange
nous *mangeons*
vous mangez
ils/elles mangent

Perfect
j'ai mangé
tu as mangé
il/elle a mangé
on a mangé
nous avons mangé
vous avez mangé
ils/elles ont mangé

Imperfect
je *mangeais*
tu *mangeais*
il/elle *mangeait*
on *mangeait*
nous mangions
vous mangiez
ils/elles *mangeaient*

Simple past
je *mangeai*
tu *mangeas*
il/elle *mangea*
on *mangea*
nous *mangeâmes*
vous *mangeâtes*
ils/elles mangèrent

Similar verbs

arranger	arrange	**juger**	judge
bouger	move	**outrager**	anger
déranger	disturb	**partager**	share
enrager	enrage	**plonger**	dive
loger	house	**ranger**	to tidy up

Notes

1. Italicized forms show the extra -e- in spelling.
2. All verbs ending in -ger are in this large group.

Present participle	Past participle
mangeant	mangé

Past perfect	Past anterior
j'avais mangé	j'eus mangé

Future	Future perfect
je mangerai	j'aurai mangé

Conditional	Conditional perfect
je mangerais	j'aurais mangé

Present subjunctive	Perfect subjunctive
que je mange	que j'aie mangé

Imperfect subjunctive	Pluperfect subjunctive
que je mangeasse	que j'eusse mangé

Il *plongea* dans la piscine et *nagea* jusqu'à l'autre bord.

He *dived* into the swimming pool and *swam* to the other side.

Une tragédie en miniature
– Qu'est-ce qu'il a, ton hamster? Il ne *bouge* plus.

A mini-tragedy
– What's the matter with your hamster? He's not *moving* any more.

– Je ne sais pas. Je voudrais bien qu'il *mange* quelque chose. La semaine dernière il *mangeait* très bien; mais depuis mardi il *n'a rien mangé* du tout.

– I don't know. I really wish he'd *eat* something. Last week he *was eating* very well; but since Tuesday he *hasn't eaten* a thing.

– Eh bien, ramasse-le! Ça ne le *dérangera* pas.

– Well, pick him up! It *won't disturb* him.

– Tu as raison. Et de toute façon il ne *rongera* plus rien. Il est mort.

– You're right. And anyway he *won't gnaw* anything else. He's dead.

7h Placer, *to put, place*
Regular -er verb ending in -cer

Imperative

place! (tu) placez! (vous) *plaçons*! (nous)

Present	**Perfect**
je place	j'ai placé
tu places	tu as placé
il/elle place	il/elle a placé
on place	on a placé
nous *plaçons*	nous avons placé
vous placez	vous avez placé
ils/elles placent	ils/elles ont placé

Imperfect	**Simple past**
je *plaçais*	je *plaçai*
tu *plaçais*	tu *plaças*
il/elle *plaçait*	il/elle *plaça*
on *plaçait*	on *plaça*
nous placions	nous *plaçâmes*
vous placiez	vous *plaçâtes*
ils/elles *plaçaient*	ils/elles placèrent

Similar verbs

annoncer	announce	**relancer**	throw back
commencer	begin	**remplacer**	replace
dénoncer	denounce	**renoncer**	renounce
effacer	rub out	**retracer**	retrace
lancer	throw; launch	**sucer**	suck
prononcer	pronounce	**tracer**	trace
recommencer	begin again		

Notes

1. The italicized forms indicate the requirement to write **ç** before vowels **a**, **o,** and **u**. Hence the cedilla is written in all parts of the imperfect indicative and imperfect subjunctive, and in the simple past except in the third-person plural; in the present participle; and in the first-person plural present tense and imperative. (Compare the parallel use of **-ge-** in verbs of the **-ger** group ➤**manger**, 7g, where exactly the same forms require the extra **-e-**.)
2. All verbs ending in **-cer** follow this pattern.

Present participle plaçant	**Past participle** placé

Past perfect j'avais placé	**Past anterior** j'eus placé
Future je placerai	**Future perfect** j'aurai placé
Conditional je placerais	**Conditional perfect** j'aurais placé
Present subjunctive que je place	**Perfect subjunctive** que j'aie placé
Imperfect subjunctive que je *plaçasse*	**Pluperfect subjunctive** que j'eusse placé

Commençons!

Let's begin!

C'est elle qui m'*a remplacé*.

She's the one who *replaced* me.

"Et la mer *efface* sur le sable les pas des amants désunis" (*Les Feuilles Mortes,* Jacques Prévert)

"And the sea *washes away* in the sand the footprints of parted lovers"

Ne *recommence* pas, je t'en supplie!

Don't *do that again*, I'm begging you.

Edward VIII *renonça* à la couronne britannique en 1938. Son frère le *remplaça*.

Edward VIII *renounced* the British crown in 1938. His brother *replaced* him.

7i   Payer, *to pay*
Regular -er verb ending in -ayer

Imperative

paye!/paie! (tu)   payez! (vous)   payons! (nous)

Present	**Perfect**
je paye/paie	j'ai payé
tu payes/paies	tu as payé
il/elle paye/paie	il/elle a payé
on paye/paie	on a payé
nous payons	nous avons payé
vous payez	vous avez payé
ils/elles payent/paient	ils/elles ont payé

Imperfect	**Simple past**
je payais	je payai
tu payais	tu payas
il/elle payait	il/elle paya
on payait	on paya
nous payions	nous payâmes
vous payiez	vous payâtes
ils/elles payaient	ils/elles payèrent

Similar verbs

déblayer	clear away	**essayer**	try
délayer	mix; thin down	**étayer**	prop up
enrayer	stop; check	**rayer**	scratch out; strike out; erase

Notes

1. Verbs in **-ayer** have always had the choice of spelling: either to keep the letter **-y-** throughout, or to have a letter **-i-** before silent **-e** (**-es**, **-ent**) in the present, future and conditional tenses.

Present participle payant	**Past participle** payé

Past perfect j'avais payé	**Past anterior** j'eus payé
Future je payerai/paierai	**Future perfect** j'aurai payé
Conditional je payerais/paierais	**Conditional perfect** j'aurais payé
Present subjunctive que je paye/paie	**Perfect subjunctive** que j'aie payé
Imperfect subjunctive que je payasse	**Pluperfect subjunctive** que j'eusse payé

Je peux *essayer* ce pantalon? May I *try* these pants *on*?

J'ai *payé* les billets, mais il faut que je *paie* le repas. I've *paid* for the tickets, but I must *pay* for the meal.

Tu *essaieras de* te mettre en contact avec lui? *Will* you *try* and contact him?

Il *a rayé* son nom. He's *crossed* his name out.

Avant de jouer au football, nous *déblayons* le terrain. Before playing soccer, we *are clearing* the ground *(of obstacles)*.

Il *délaie* son discours en donnant beaucoup d'exemples. He's *spinning out* his speech by giving lots of examples.

-ir verbs

8a Finir, *to finish*
Regular -ir verb

Imperative
finis! (tu)   finissez! (vous)   finissons! (nous)

Present	Perfect
je finis	j'ai fini
tu finis	tu as fini
il/elle finit	il/elle a fini
on finit	on a fini
nous finissons	nous avons fini
vous finissez	vous avez fini
ils/elles finissent	ils/elles ont fini

Imperfect	Simple past
je finissais	je finis
tu finissais	tu finis
il/elle finissait	il/elle finit
on finissait	on finit
nous finissions	nous finîmes
vous finissiez	vous finîtes
ils/elles finissaient	ils/elles finirent

Past perfect	Past anterior
j'avais fini	j'eus fini
tu avais fini	tu eus fini
il/elle avait fini	il/elle eut fini
on avait fini	on eut fini
nous avions fini	nous eûmes fini
vous aviez fini	vous eûtes fini
ils/elles avaient fini	ils/elles eurent fini

Present participle	Past participle
finissant	fini

Future	Future perfect
je finirai	j'aurai fini
tu finiras	tu auras fini
il/elle finira	il/elle aura fini
on finira	on aura fini
nous finirons	nous aurons fini
vous finirez	vous aurez fini
ils/elles finiront	ils/elles auront fini

Conditional	Conditional perfect
je finirais	j'aurais fini
tu finirais	tu aurais fini
il/elle finirait	il/elle aurait
on finirait	on aurait fini
nous finirions	nous aurions fini
vous finiriez	vous auriez fini
ils/elles finiraient	ils/elles auraient fini

Present subjunctive	Perfect subjunctive
que je finisse	que j'aie fini
que tu finisses	que tu aies fini
qu'il/elle finisse	qu'il/elle ait fini
qu'on finisse	qu'on ait fini
que nous finissions	que nous ayons fini
que vous finissiez	que vous ayez fini
qu'ils/elles finissent	qu'ils/elles aient fini

Imperfect subjunctive	Pluperfect subjunctive
que je finisse	que j'eusse fini
que tu finisses	que tu eusses fini
qu'il/elle finît	qu'il/elle eût fini
qu'on finît	qu'on eût fini
que nous finissions	que nous eussions fini
que vous finissiez	que vous eussiez fini
qu'ils/elles finissent	qu'ils/elles eussent fini

Similar verbs

accomplir	achieve	**franchir**	cross
amortir	deaden; cushion	**réfléchir**	reflect; ponder
applaudir	applaud	**réussir**	succeed
avertir	warn	**surgir**	appear suddenly
choisir	choose		

Change-of-state verbs

appauvrir	impoverish	**jaunir**	go yellow
blanchir	turn white	**réunir**	gather together
démolir	demolish	**rougir**	go red
enrichir	enrich	**vieillir**	grow old
établir	establish	**unir**	unite
guérir	cure; heal		

Notes

1. The regular **-ir** conjugation with **-iss-** is a large group.
2. It includes verbs implying some kind of development or change of state.

Au rayon des disques
– Les enfants, je vous *avertis* qu'on part dans deux minutes.
– Oh maman! je n'*ai* pas *fini.* Je n'*ai* rien *choisi.*
– Et moi, maman? Il faut que je *réfléchisse!* Trouver un cadeau pour Papa, ce n'est pas facile.
– Eh bien, on n'*a* pas *accompli* grand-chose ce matin.
– C'est vrai, mais si le prof ne m'*avait* pas *puni,* on aurait eu beaucoup plus de temps pour *choisir.*

On *avait établi* un petit commerce, mais cela n'*a* pas *réussi.*

Les moteurs de l'avion *vrombissaient* au décollage.

Je ne voudrais pas qu'on *démolisse* le vieux musée.

At the record counter
– Children, I'*m warning* you that we're leaving in two minutes.
– Oh Mom, I *haven't finished.* I *haven't chosen* anything.
– And what about me, Mom? I have to *think about this.* Finding a present for Dad isn't easy.
– Well, we *haven't achieved* much this morning.
– That's true, but if the teacher *hadn't punished* me, we would have had a lot more time *to choose.*

They *had set up* a small business, but it *didn't succeed.*

The plane's engines *were roaring* on takeoff.

I wouldn't like them to *knock down* the old museum.

8b   Acquérir, *to acquire*
Irregular -ir verb

Imperative
acquiers! (tu)   acquérez! (vous)   acquérons! (nous)

Present
j'acquiers
tu acquiers
il/elle acquiert
on acquiert
nous acquérons
vous acquérez
ils/elles acquièrent

Perfect
j'ai acquis
tu as acquis
il/elle a acquis
on a acquis
nous avons acquis
vous avez acquis
ils/elles ont acquis

Imperfect
j'acquérais
tu acquérais
il/elle acquérait
on acquérait
nous acquérions
vous acquériez
ils/elles acquéraient

Simple past
j'acquis
tu acquis
il/elle acquit
on acquit
nous acquîmes
vous acquîtes
ils/elles acquirent

Similar verbs

conquérir   conquer   **reconquérir**   reconquer

Notes

1. The main difficulties in this verb are in the present tenses, as well as the future and conditional.

J'*ai acquis* cette table chez un brocanteur.

I *acquired* this table at a secondhand dealer's.

Où veux-tu que j'*acquière* un vélo à cette heure-ci?

Where do you expect me to *get* a bike from at this time of day?

Present participle	**Past participle**
acquérant	acquis

Past perfect	**Past anterior**
j'avais acquis	j'eus acquis

Future
j'acquerrai

Future perfect
j'aurai acquis

Conditional
j'acquerrais

Conditional perfect
j'aurais acquis

Present subjunctive
que j'acquière
que tu acquières
qu'il/elle acquière
qu'on acquière
que nous acquérions
que vous acquériez
qu'ils/elles acquièrent

Perfect subjunctive
que j'aie acquis

Imperfect subjunctive
que j'acquisse

Pluperfect subjunctive
que j'eusse acquis

Jules César *conquit* la
Gaule en 58 av.J-C.

Julius Caesar *conquered*
Gaul in 58 B.C.

Tu *acquerras* des tableaux?

Will you *purchase* some paintings?

Ces antiquités *ont acquis*
beaucoup de valeur.

These antiques *have
appreciated* a lot in value.

Ce Lothario *conquiert* tous
les coeurs des dames.

That Lothario *wins* all the
ladies' hearts.

Sans la trahison, nous
aurions reconquis notre liberté.

If we hadn't been betrayed, we
would have won back our freedom.

8c   Cueillir, *to pick*
Irregular -ir verb

Imperative
cueille! (tu)   *cueillez!* (vous)   *cueillons!* (nous)

Present
je *cueille*
tu *cueilles*
il/elle cueille
on cueille
nous cueillons
vous cueillez
ils/elles cueillent

Perfect
j'ai cueilli
tu as cueilli
il/elle a cueilli
on a cueilli
nous avons cueilli
vous avez cueilli
ils/elles ont cueilli

Imperfect
je *cueillais*
tu *cueillais*
il/elle *cueillait*
on *cueillait*
nous *cueillions*
vous *cueilliez*
ils/elles *cueillaient*

Simple past
je cueillis
tu cueillis
il/elle cueillit
on cueillit
nous cueillîmes
vous cueillîtes
ils/elles cueillirent

Similar verbs

acceillir	welcome	**recueillir**	pick again

Notes

1. Italicized forms show differences from regular **-ir** verbs.
2. This group, like the **ouvrir** group, has a mixture of forms from the **-er** and **-ir** conjugations.
3. **Assaillir** (to assail) and **défaillir** (to faint, falter) are conjugated like **cueillir** in all forms except the future and conditional tenses, where the form is **j'assaillirai**.

"*Cueillez* **dès aujourd'hui les roses de la vie.**" (*Ronsard, sixteenth century*)	Gather ye rosebuds while ye may. (*Literally, "Gather the roses of life today."*)
Voici les pommes que j'*ai* **cueillies ce matin.**	These are the apples I *picked* this morning.

Present participle cueillant	**Past participle** cueilli
Past perfect j'avais cueilli	**Past anterior** j'eus cueilli
Future je *cueillerai* tu *cueilleras*	**Future perfect** j'aurai cueilli
Conditional je *cueillerais*	**Conditional perfect** j'aurais cueilli
Present subjunctive que je *cueille*	**Perfect subjunctive** que j'aie cueilli
Imperfect subjunctive que je cueillisse	**Pluperfect subjunctive** que j'eusse cueilli

L'hôtel peut *accueillir* un grand nombre de touristes.	The hotel can *accommodate* a large number of tourists.
On m'*a accueilli* avec chaleur.	They *welcomed* me warmly.
Je l'*accueillerai* chez moi.	I *shall welcome* him into my home.
Dans six mois; il *aura recueilli* son héritage.	In six months he *will have come into* his inheritance.
Le compositeur Vaughan Williams *recueillait* régulièrement les vieilles chansons folkloriques qu'il entendait.	The composer Vaughan Williams regularly *noted down* the old folk songs he heard.
On l'*a assailli* de questions après le discours.	They *bombarded* him with questions after the speech.
Elle *défaille* de faim.	She's *fainting* with hunger.

8d   Courir, *to run*
Irregular -ir verb

Imperative
cours! (tu)   courez! (vous)   courons! (nous)

Present	Perfect
je cours	j'ai couru
tu cours	tu as couru
il/elle court	il/elle a couru
on court	on a couru
nous courons	nous avons couru
vous courez	vous avez couru
ils/elles courent	ils/elles ont couru

Imperfect	Simple past
je courais	je courus
tu courais	tu courus
il/elle courait	il/elle courut
on courait	on courut
nous courions	nous courûmes
vous couriez	vous courûtes
ils/elles couraient	ils/elles coururent

Similar verbs

accourir	run up; rush up	**recourir**	run again
concourir	compete	**secourir**	help; assist
parcourir	cover; travel		

Present participle	**Present participle**
courant	couru

Past perfect	**Past anterior**
j'avais couru	j'eus couru
Future	**Future perfect**
je courrai	j'aurai couru
Conditional	**Conditional perfect**
je courrais	j'aurais couru
Present subjunctive	**Perfect subjunctive**
que je coure	que j'aie couru
Imperfect subjunctive	**Pluperfect subjunctive**
que je courusse	que j'eusse couru

J'*ai couru*. Je suis essoufflé.	I'*ve been running*. I'm out of breath.
Allez, *courez!*	Come on, *run!*
Il *a parcouru* le monde.	He'*s been* all over the world.
Je *recourrai* au patron.	I *shall appeal* to the boss.
On *aurait concouru* à ce projet, mais l'argent manquait.	We *would have cooperated* on that project, but money was short.
Il *secourait* toujours les amis qui avaient des problèmes financiers.	He *always helped* friends who had financial problems.

8e   Dormir, *to sleep*

Irregular -ir verb

Imperative

dors! (tu)   *dormez!* (vous)   *dormons!* (nous)

Present	**Perfect**
je *dors*	j'ai dormi
tu *dors*	tu as dormi
il/elle *dort*	il/elle a dormi
on *dort*	on a dormi
nous *dormons*	nous avons dormi
vous *dormez*	vous avez dormi
ils/elles *dorment*	ils/elles ont dormi

Imperfect	**Simple past**
je *dormais*	je dormis
tu *dormais*	tu dormis
il/elle *dormait*	il/elle dormit
on *dormait*	on dormit
nous *dormions*	nous dormîmes
vous *dormiez*	vous dormîtes
ils/elles *dormaient*	ils/elles dormirent

Similar verbs

s'endormir   go to sleep   **se rendormir**   go back to sleep

Notes

1. Italicized forms show differences from model verb **finir** (➤8a).

– *Avez*-vous bien *dormi?*	– Did you sleep well?
– Oui, je *me suis* très vite *endormi*. Mais mon mari ne *dort* jamais bien.	– Yes *I went to sleep* very quickly. But my husband never *sleeps* well.
– Il s'est réveillé pendant la nuit?	– Did he wake up in the night?
– Oui, et il ne *s'est* pas *rendormi* avant six heures.	– *Yes*, and he didn't *get back* to sleep until six o'clock.

Present participle	Past participle
dormant	dormi

Past perfect	Past anterior
j'avais dormi	j'eus dormi

Future	Future perfect
je dormirai	j'aurai dormi

Conditional	Conditional perfect
je dormirais	j'aurais dormi

Present subjunctive	Perfect subjunctive
que je *dorme*	que j'aie dormi

Imperfect subjunctive	Pluperfect subjunctive
que je dormisse	que j'eusse dormi

Dormez bien, les enfants!

Sleep well, children.

Tu *dormiras* bien après un petit verre de cognac.

You'*ll sleep* well after a small glass of brandy.

Ne faites pas de bruit – les gosses *se seront endormis!*

Don't make a noise – the kids *will have gone to sleep.*

On *se serait rendormis* s'il n'y avait pas eu tous ces trains qui passaient.

We *would have gone back to sleep* if all those trains hadn't been going by.

Elle *s'était* vite *endormie.*

She *had fallen asleep* quickly.

8f   Faillir, *to almost do, to fail*
Irregular -ir verb

Imperative
—

Present	**Perfect**
—	j'ai failli
	tu as failli
	il/elle a failli
	on a failli
	nous avons failli
	vous avez failli
	ils/elles ont failli

Imperfect	**Simple past**
—	je faillis
	tu faillis
	il/elle faillit
	on faillit
	nous faillîmes
	vous faillîtes
	ils/elles faillirent

Notes

1. This verb exists only in past tenses.

Present participle	Past participle
faillant	failli

Past perfect	Past anterior
j'avais failli	j'eus failli

Future	Future perfect
—	j'aurai failli

Conditional	Conditional perfect
—	j'aurais failli

Present subjunctive	Perfect subjunctive
—	que j'aie failli

Imperfect subjunctive	Pluperfect subjunctive
—	que j'eusse failli

J'*ai failli* réussir.	I *almost* succeeded.
Il *a failli* tomber.	He *almost* fell.
On *a failli* perdre tout notre argent.	We *nearly* lost all our money.

Notes

1. The idiom **faillir à quelque chose** means "to be lacking, to fail in something."

Il *faillit* à son devoir.	He *failed* in his duty.
Son courage lui *faillit*.	Her courage *failed* her.

8g   Fuir, *to flee*
Irregular -ir verb

Imperative
fuis! (tu)   fuyez! (vous)   fuyons! (nous)

Present	**Perfect**
je fuis	j'ai fui
tu fuis	tu as fui
il/elle fuit	il/elle a fui
on fuit	on a fui
nous fuyons	nous avons fui
vous fuyez	vous avez fui
ils/elles fuient	ils/elles ont fui

Imperfect	**Simple past**
je fuyais	je fuis
tu fuyais	tu fuis
il/elle fuyait	il/elle fuit
on fuyait	on fuit
nous fuyions	nous fuîmes
vous fuyiez	vous fuîtes
ils/elles fuyaient	ils/elles fuirent

Similar verbs

s'enfuir   run away; flee

Notes

1. The **-y-** in forms with an audible ending is the main feature of this verb.
2. **S'enfuir** (flee from; run away) is conjugated in the same way (with **être** in compound tenses).

Present participle	**Past participle**
fuyant	fui

Past perfect	**Past anterior**
j'avais fui	j'eus fui

Future	**Future perfect**
je fuirai	j'aurai fui

Conditional	**Conditional perfect**
je fuirais	j'aurais fui

Present subjunctive	**Perfect subjunctive**
que je fuie	que j'aie fui

Imperfect subjunctive	**Pluperfect subjunctive**
que je fuisse	que j'eusse fui

Fuyons!	Let's *run for it!*
Il *s'est enfui* à toute vitesse.	He *ran away* as fast as he could.
Les réfugiés *fuient* devant les soldats.	The refugees *are fleeing* from the soldiers.
Le temps *fuit*.	Time *flies*.
Le beau temps *a fui*.	The fine weather'*s gone*.

8h   Mourir, *to die*
Irregular -ir verb

Imperative
meurs! (tu)   mourez! (vous)   mourons! (nous)

Present
je meurs
tu meurs
il/elle meurt
on meurt
nous mourons
vous mourez
ils/elles meurent

Perfect
je suis mort
tu es mort
il est mort/elle est morte
on est mort
nous sommes morts
vous êtes mort(-e/-s/-es)
ils sont morts/elles sont mortes

Imperfect
je mourais
tu mourais
il/elle mourait
on mourait
nous mourions
vous mouriez
ils/elles mouraient

Simple past
je mourus
tu mourus
il/elle mourut
on mourut
nous mourûmes
vous mourûtes
ils/elles moururent

Notes
1. The present tenses and the future and conditional, as well as the simple past and imperfect subjunctive, are irregular forms.
2. The past participle is irregular but well known in its use as the adjective "dead."
3. **Mourir** takes **être** in compound tenses, as does **naître** (to be born).

Il *est mort*.	He is *dead/has died*.
Jeanne d'Arc *mourut* en 1431.	Joan of Arc *died* in 1431.
On *a failli mourir* de peur.	We *nearly died* of fright.
C'est *à mourir* de rire.	It's *enough to make you die* laughing.
Il *devait mourir* plus tard de ses blessures.	He *was to die* later from his wounds.
On attend qu'il *meure*.	We're waiting for him to *die*.

Present participle	***Past participle***
mourant	mort

Past perfect	***Past anterior***
j'étais mort(-e)	je fus mort(-e)
Future	***Future perfect***
je mourrai	je serai mort(-e)
Conditional	***Conditional perfect***
je mourrais	je serais mort(-e)
Present subjunctive	***Perfect subjunctive***
que je meure	que je sois mort(-e)
Imperfect subjunctive	***Pluperfect subjunctive***
que je mourusse	que je fusse mort(-e)

Sans les soins de mon médicin, je *serais mort* il y a bien longtemps.	Without my doctor's care, I *would have died* ages ago.
Bien des enfants du Tiers Monde *meurent* avant l'âge de cinq ans.	Many children in the Third World *die* before the age of five.
Quelle tragédie que Chopin *soit mort* si jeune!	What a tragedy that Chopin *died* so young!

8i   Ouvrir, *to open*
Irregular -ir verb

Imperative

ouvre! (tu)   *ouvrez!* (vous)   *ouvrons!* (nous)

Present
j'*ouvre*
tu *ouvres*
il/elle *ouvre*
on *ouvre*
nous *ouvrons*
vous *ouvrez*
ils/elles *ouvrent*

Perfect
j'ai *ouvert*
tu as *ouvert*
il/elle a *ouvert*
on a *ouvert*
nous avons *ouvert*
vous avez *ouvert*
ils/elles ont *ouvert*

Imperfect
j'*ouvrais*
tu *ouvrais*
il/elle *ouvrait*
on *ouvrait*
nous *ouvrions*
vous *ouvriez*
ils/elles *ouvraient*

Simple past
j'ouvris
tu ouvris
il/elle ouvrit
on ouvrit
nous ouvrîmes
vous ouvrîtes
ils/elles ouvrirent

Similar verbs

couvrir	cover	**rouvrir**	open again
découvrir	discover	**souffrir**	suffer
offrir	offer		

Notes

1. Italicized forms show differences from model verb **finir** (➤8a).
2. This group displays a mixture of forms from the **-er** and **-ir** conjugations.

Present participle	**Past participle**
ouvrant	ouvert

Past perfect	**Past anterior**
j'avais *ouvert*	j'eus *ouvert*
Future	**Future perfect**
j'ouvrirai	j'aurai *ouvert*
Conditional	**Conditional perfect**
j'ouvrirais	j'aurais *ouvert*
Present subjunctive	**Perfect subjunctive**
que j'*ouvre*	que j'aie *ouvert*
que tu *ouvres*	
Imperfect subjunctive	**Pluperfect subjunctive**
que j'ouvrisse	que j'eusse *ouvert*

***Ouvrez* les fenêtres!**	*Open* the windows!
Qu'est-ce qu'on t'*a offert* comme cadeau?	What present *did* they *give* you?
D'ici on *découvre* toute la ville.	You *can see* the whole town from here.
La police *a découvert* deux kilos de cannabis dans la voiture.	The police *discovered* two kilos of cannabis in the car.
Va *ouvrir*!	Go and *open* the door!
Le bureau *ouvre* à quelle heure?	What time *does* the office *open*?
Il nous *offrait* de séjourner chez lui.	He *offered* to put us up at his place. (Literally, *He was offering us a stay at his house.*)
Maintenant il *aura découvert* son erreur.	He *will have discovered* his mistake by now.

8j   Sentir, *to feel*
Irregular -ir verb

Imperative

sens! (tu)   *sentez!* (vous)   *sentons!* (nous)

Present	**Perfect**
je *sens*	j'ai senti
tu *sens*	tu as senti
il/elle *sent*	il/elle a senti
on *sent*	on a senti
nous *sentons*	nous avons senti
vous *sentez*	vous avez senti
ils/elles *sentent*	ils/elles ont senti

Imperfect	**Simple past**
je *sentais*	je sentis
tu *sentais*	tu sentis
il/elle *sentait*	il/elle sentit
on *sentait*	on sentit
nous *sentions*	nous sentîmes
vous *sentiez*	vous sentîtes
ils/elles *sentaient*	ils/elles sentirent

Similar verbs

mentir	lie; tell lies	**se repentir**	repent
partir	leave; go away	**sortir**	go out
ressentir	feel; experience		

Notes

1. Italicized forms show differences from model verb **finir** (➤8a).
2. **Sortir** and **partir**, plus their compounds, are also in this group, though these are all conjugated with **être** in compound tenses.

Present participle	Past participle
sentant	senti

Past perfect	Past anterior
j'avais senti	j'eus senti

Future	Future perfect
je sentirai	j'aurai senti

Conditional	Conditional perfect
je sentirais	j'aurais senti

Present subjunctive	Perfect subjunctive
que je *sente*	que j'aie senti
que tu *sentes*	
qu'il/elle *sente*	

Imperfect subjunctive	Pluperfect subjunctive
que je sentisse	que j'eusse senti

Je ne *me sens* pas très bien aujourd'hui.	I don't *feel* very well today.
Ce n'est pas vrai – tu m'*as menti*.	It isn't true – you *lied* to me.
. . . il est permis de *mentir* aux enfants quand c'est pour leur bien. *La Gloire de mon père* (Marcel Pagnol)	. . . you are allowed *to lie* to children when it's for their own good.
"*Repens-toi*, Dieu te pardonnera!" *(Line from traditional song about St Nicholas)*	"*Repent*, God will forgive you!"
Il *est sorti* tout à l'heure.	He just *went out*.
Le bateau *partira* à quatorze heures.	The boat *will leave* at 2:00 P.M.

8k   Tenir, *to hold*
Irregular -ir verb

Imperative

tiens! (tu)   tenez! (vous)   tenons! (nous)

Present	**Perfect**
je tiens	j'ai tenu
tu tiens	tu as tenu
il/elle tient	il/elle a tenu
on tient	on a tenu
nous tenons	nous avons tenu
vous tenez	vous avez tenu
ils/elles tiennent	ils/elles ont tenu

Imperfect	**Simple past**
je tenais	je tins
tu tenais	tu tins
il/elle tenait	il/elle tint
on tenait	on tint
nous tenions	nous tînmes
vous teniez	vous tîntes
ils/elles tenaient	ils/elles tinrent

Past perfect	**Past anterior**
j'avais tenu	j'eus tenu

Similar verbs

abstenir (s')	refrain; abstain	**maintenir**	maintain
appartenir	belong	**obtenir**	obtain
contenir	contain; hold; take	**retenir**	hold back
détenir	detain; hold	**soutenir**	support;
entretenir	maintain; keep; support		sustain

Notes

1. **Venir** and all its compounds are also in this group, but are conjugated with **être** in compound tenses (except **prévenir**, which is conjugated with **avoir**). Compounds are **convenir**; **devenir**; **intervenir**; **souvenir (se)**; **survenir**; and **redevenir**.
2. **Venir de faire** is an idiomatic expression meaning "to have done."

Present participle	**Past participle**
tenant	tenu

Future	**Future perfect**
je tiendrai	j'aurai tenu

Conditional	**Conditional perfect**
je tiendrais	j'aurais tenu

Present subjunctive

que je tienne
que tu tiennes
qu'il/elle tienne
qu'on tienne
que nous tenions
que vous teniez
qu'ils/elles tiennent

Perfect subjunctive

que j'aie tenu

Imperfect subjunctive

que je tinsse
que tu tinsses
qu'il tînt
que nous tinssions
que vous tinssiez
qu'ils/elles tinssent

Pluperfect subjunctive

que j'eusse tenu

Tu *viens* avec moi?	*Are* you *coming* with me?
Il *tenait à* faire votre connaissance.	He really *wanted to* meet you.
Il *est devenu* facteur.	He *became* a mailman.
Demain elle va *soutenir* sa thèse.	Tomorrow she's going to defend her thesis.
Je ne sais pas ce qui *me retient* de vous casser la figure. La Gloire de mon père (Marcel Pagnol)	I don't know what's *stopping* me from smashing your face in.

Examples of the use of **venir de faire:**

Le train *venait de partir.*	The train *had just left.*
'*Vient de paraître*'.	*Just out/just published.*

81 Vêtir, *to dress*
Irregular -ir verb

Imperative

vêts! (tu)　　　　vêtez! (vous)　　　　vêtons! (nous)

Present
je vêts
tu vêts
il/elle vêt
on vêt
nous vêtons
vous vêtez
ils/elles vêtent

Perfect
j'ai vêtu
tu as vêtu
il/elle a vêtu
on a vêtu
nous avons vêtu
vous avez vêtu
ils/elles ont vêtu

Imperfect
je vêtais
tu vêtais
il/elle vêtait
on vêtait
nous vêtions
vous vêtiez
ils/elles vêtaient

Simple past
je vêtis
tu vêtis
il/elle vêtit
on vêtit
nous vêtîmes
vous vêtîtes
ils/elles vêtirent

Similar verbs

dévêtir　　　undress　　　**revêtir**　　　put on; take on

Notes

1. The reflexive verb means "to get dressed," and is more usual with compound tenses conjugated with **être**, in common with all reflexive verbs.

Present participle vêtant	**Past participle** vêtu

Past participle j'avais vêtu	**Past anterior** j'eus vêtu
Future je vêtirai	**Future perfect** j'aurai vêtu
Conditional je vêtirais	**Conditional perfect** j'aurais vêtu
Present subjunctive que je vête	**Perfect subjunctive** que j'aie vêtu
Imperfect subjunctive que je vêtisse	**Pluperfect subjunctive** que j'eusse vêtu

Elle *s'est vêtue* en noir.   She *dressed* in black.

***Revêts-toi* vite!**   Quick! *Put your clothes back on!*

-re verbs

9a Vendre, *to sell*
Regular -re verb

Imperative
vends! (tu)   vendez! (vous)   vendons! (nous)

Present
je vends
tu vends
il/elle vend
on vend
nous vendons
vous vendez
ils/elles vendent

Perfect
j'ai vendu
tu as vendu
il/elle a vendu
on a vendu
nous avons vendu
vous avez vendu
ils/elles ont vendu

Imperfect
je vendais
tu vendais
il/elle vendait
on vendait
nous vendions
vous vendiez
ils/elles vendaient

Simple past
je vendis
tu vendis
il/elle vendit
on vendit
nous vendîmes
vous vendîtes
ils/elles vendirent

Past perfect
j'avais vendu
tu avais vendu
il/elle avait vendu
on avait vendu
nous avions vendu
vous aviez vendu
ils/elles avaient vendu

Past anterior
j'eus vendu
tu eus vendu
il/elle eut vendu
on eut vendu
nous eûmes vendu
vous eûtes vendu
ils/elles eurent vendu

Present participle	*Future perfect*
vendant	vendu

Future
je vendrai
tu vendras
il/elle vendra
on vendra
nous vendrons
vous vendrez
ils/elles vendront

Future perfect
j'aurai vendu
tu auras vendu
il/elle aura vendu
on aura vendu
nous aurons vendu
vous aurez vendu
ils/elles auront vendu

Conditional
je vendrais
tu vendrais
il/elle vendrait
on vendrait
nous vendrions
vous vendriez
ils/elles vendraient

Conditional perfect
j'aurais vendu
tu aurais vendu
il/elle aurait vendu
on aurait vendu
nous aurions vendu
vous auriez vendu
ils/elles auraient vendu

Present subjunctive
que je vende
que tu vendes
qu'il/elle vende
qu'on vende
que nous vendions
que vous vendiez
qu'ils/elles vendent

Perfect subjunctive
que j'aie vendu
que tu aies vendu
qu'il/elle ait vendu
qu'on ait vendu
que nous ayons vendu
que vous ayez vendu
qu'ils/elles aient vendu

Imperfect subjunctive
que je vendisse
que tu vendisses
qu'il/elle vendît
qu'on vendît
que nous vendissions
que vous vendissiez
qu'ils/elles vendissent

Pluperfect subjunctive
que j'eusse vendu
que tu eusses vendu
qu'il/elle eût vendu
qu'on eût vendu
que nous eussions vendu
que vous eussiez vendu
qu'ils/elles eussent vendu

Similar verbs

attendre	wait (for)	**prétendre**	claim
dépendre	depend	**répandre**	spread
descendre	to come/go down;	**répondre**	answer
	to take down	**rendre**	give back, render
entendre	hear	**suspendre**	hang, suspend
pendre	hang	**tondre**	cut (lawn)
pondre	lay (eggs)		

Notes

1. A large group of verbs follows this pattern of the regular **-re** conjugation.

2. There are, however, a lot of verbs with infinitives in **-re** which are irregular.

3. **Rompre** (to break) is conjugated like **vendre**, except that the third person singular of the present tense is **il rompt**, etc. Compounds **corrompre** (to corrupt, taint) and **interrompre** (to interrupt) follow this pattern.

4. **Vaincre** (to win, conquer) is conjugated like **vendre**, except that it requires **-qu-** in the plural of the present indicative and in all parts of the imperfect tenses, the simple past and the present subjunctive. **Convaincre** (to convince) has the same forms.

5. **Descendre** can be used as an inhansitive verb, using **être** as its auxilliary, or as a transitive verb, using **avoir** as its auxilliary.

– **Qu'est-ce que vous *attendez*?**

– What are you *waiting for?*

– **J'*ai entendu dire* qu'on allait vendre des cassettes et des CD ici au marché.**

– I've heard they're going to sell cassettes and CDs here in the market.

– **C'*est* vrai? A quelle heure?**

– *Is* that right? What time?

– **Je ne sais pas. Ça *dépend* . . .**

– I don't know. It *depends* . . .

– **Nous *descendions de* l'autobus quand le gangster l'*a descendu*.**

– We *were getting off* the bus when the gangster *shot* him *dead*. (*Literally, "felled him," "took him down."*)

9b   Boire, *to drink*
Irregular -re verb

Imperative
bois! (tu)   buvez! (vous)   buvons! (nous)

Present	Perfect
je bois	j'ai bu
tu bois	tu as bu
il/elle boit	il/elle a bu
on boit	on a bu
nous buvons	nous avons bu
vous buvez	vous avez bu
ils/elles boivent	ils/elles ont bu

Imperfect	Simple past
je buvais	je bus
tu buvais	tu bus
il/elle buvait	il/elle but
on buvait	on but
nous buvions	nous bûmes
vous buviez	vous bûtes
ils/elles buvaient	ils/elles burent

Notes

1. This is the only verb of its type.

Present participle	*Past participle*
buvant	bu

Past perfect	*Past anterior*
j'avais bu	j'eus bu
Future	*Future perfect*
je boirai	j'aurai bu
Conditional	*Conditional perfect*
je boirais	j'aurais bu
Present subjunctive	*Perfect subjunctive*
que je boive	que j'aie bu
Imperfect subjunctive	*Pluperfect subjunctive*
que je busse	que j'eusse bu

J'en *boirai* cinq ou six bouteilles (Traditional song *Chevaliers de la table ronde*)	I'*ll drink* five or six bottles . . .
Il *a* trop *bu*.	He'*s had* too much to *drink*.
Tu *bois* du thé?	*Do* you *drink* tea?
Je ne *bois* pas d'alcool.	I *don't drink* alcohol.
Tant il *but* et mangea, le pauvre saint homme, qu'il mourut pendant la nuit . . .	So much *did* he eat and *drink*, the poor holy man, that he died during the night . . .
Allons boire un petit coup. *(Lettres de mon moulin*, Alphonse Daudet)	Let's go and have a drink

9c   Conclure, *to conclude*
Irregular -re verb

Imperative

conclus! (tu)   concluez! (vous)   concluons! (nous)

Present	**Perfect**
je conclus	j'ai conclu
tu conclus	tu as conclu
il/elle conclut	il/elle a conclu
on conclut	on a conclu
nous concluons	nous avons conclu
vous concluez	vous avez conclu
ils/elles concluent	ils/elles ont conclu

Imperfect	**Simple past**
je concluais	je conclus
tu concluais	tu conclus
il/elle concluait	il/elle conclut
on concluait	on conclut
nous concluions	nous conclûmes
vous concluiez	vous conclûtes
ils/elles concluaient	ils/elles conclurent

Similar verbs

exclure   turn out, put out   **inclure**   insert, include

Notes

1. **Inclure** (to insert, include) is conjugated like **conclure**, the only differences being that the past participle is **inclus**.

Present participle	Past participle
concluant	conclu

Past perfect	Past anterior
j'avais conclu	j'eus conclu

Future	Future perfect
je conclurai	j'aurai conclu

Conditional	Conditional perfect
je conclurais	j'aurais conclu

Present subjunctive	Perfect subjunctive
que je conclue	que j'aie conclu

Imperfect subjunctive	Pluperfect subjunctive
que je conclusse	que j'eusse conclu

Marché *conclu!*	It's a deal!
Les jurés *ont conclu* à sa culpabilité.	The jury *decided* he was guilty.
Vous trouverez *ci-inclus* le dossier que j'ai préparé.	You will find *enclosed* the file I prepared.
On *conclut* le traité de Versailles en 1919.	The treaty of Versailles *was signed* in 1919.
J'*ai conclu* mon article en donnant des statistiques.	I'*ve concluded* my article by giving some statistics.
On *exclut* votre participation à ce projet.	They *are refusing* to let you join in this project.
Il n'*est* pas *exclu* que je fasse partie du groupe.	It's not *out of the question* for me to join the group.

9d Conduire, *to drive, lead*
Irregular -re verb ending in -uire

Imperative

conduis! (tu)   conduisez! (vous)   conduisons! (nous)

Present	**Perfect**
je conduis	j'ai conduit
tu conduis	tu as conduit
il/elle conduit	il/elle a conduit
on conduit	on a conduit
nous conduisons	nous avons conduit
vous conduisez	vous avez conduit
ils/elles conduisent	ils/elles ont conduit

Imperfect	**Simple past**
je conduisais	je conduisis
tu conduisais	tu conduisis
il/elle conduisait	il/elle conduisit
on conduisait	on conduisit
nous conduisions	nous conduisîmes
vous conduisiez	vous conduisîtes
ils/elles conduisaient	ils/elles conduisirent

Similar verbs

construire	construct; build	**nuire**	harm
cuire	cook	**produire**	produce
introduire	introduce	**réduire**	reduce
luire	gleam; shine	**traduire**	translate

Notes

1. Verbs in this group include compounds of the verbs listed here (e.g., **reconstruire**, "to reconstruct.")
2. The past participles of **luire** and **nuire** are **lui** and **nui**.

Au restaurant	**At the restaurant**
– Et le steak, vous le *prenez* comment?	– How would you *like* your steak?
– Bien *cuit*.	– Well *done*.

Present participle	**Past participle**
conduisant	conduit

Past perfect	**Past anterior**
j'avais conduit	j'eus conduit
Future	**Future perfect**
je conduirai	j'aurai conduit
Conditional	**Conditional perfect**
je conduirais	j'aurais conduit
Present subjunctive	**Perfect subjunctive**
que je conduise	que j'aie conduit
Imperfect subjunctive	**Pluperfect subjunctive**
que je conduisisse	que j'eusse conduit

– Tiens! Je ne savais pas qu'on *avait construit* cet immeuble!
– Oui, c'est une compagnie italienne qui l'*a construit* et c'est moi qui *ai traduit* touts les documents.
– Ah bon? Mais tu *conduis* trop vite, tu sais.

– Wow! I didn't know they'*d built* that apartment house.
– Yes, it's an Italian company that *built it*, and I was the one who *translated* all the documents.
– Oh yes? But you'*re driving* too fast, you know.

– Quelle est cette lumière qui *luit* là-bas?
– Je crois que c'est l'aurore boréale que *produit* ces couleurs.

– What's that light *glowing* over there?
– I think it's the aurora borealis that's producing those colors.

9e   Connaître, *to know*
Irregular -re verb

Imperative

connais! (tu)   connaissez! (vous)   connaissons! (nous)

Present	**Perfect**
je connais	j'ai connu
tu connais	tu as connu
il/elle connaît	il/elle a connu
on connaît	on a connu
nous connaissons	nous avons connu
vous connaissez	vous avez connu
ils connaissent	ils/elles ont connu

Imperfect	**Simple past**
je connaissais	je connus
tu connaissais	tu connus
il/elle connaissait	il/elle connut
on connaissait	on connut
nous connaissions	nous connûmes
vous connaissiez	vous connûtes
ils/elles connaissaient	ils/elles connurent

Similar verbs

apparaître	appear
comparaître	appear (in court)
disparaître	disappear
paraître	to seem, appear
reconnaître	recognize

Notes

1. All compounds of **connaître** and **paraître** follow the pattern of **connaître**.

Present participle	*Past participle*
connaissant	connu

Past perfect	*Past anterior*
j'avais connu	j'eus connu
Future	*Future perfect*
je connaîtrai	j'aurai connu
Conditional	*Conditional perfect*
je connaîtrais	j'aurais connu
Present subjunctive	*Perfect subjunctive*
que je connaisse	que j'aie connu
Imperfect subjunctive	*Pluperfect subjunctive*
que je connusse	que j'eusse connu

Les causes de ce désastre ne *sont* **pas encore** *connues.*	The causes of this disaster *are*n't yet *known.*
Tu *connais* **cet homme?**	*Do* you *know* that man?
Il l'*a connue* **à Paris.**	He *met* her in Paris.
Je la *connaissais* **déjà depuis cinq ans.**	I'*d* already *known* her for five years.
Il doit *comparaître* **devant le tribunal.**	He has *to appear* before the court.
Il *parait* **qu' ils** *s'étaient connus* **. . .**	It *seems* that they *had got to know each other* . . .

9f   Coudre, *to sew*
Irregular -re verb

Imperative

couds! (tu)   cousez! (vous)   cousons! (nous)

Present
je couds
tu couds
il/elle coud
on coud
nous cousons
vous cousez
ils/elles cousent

Perfect
j'ai cousu
tu as cousu
il/elle a cousu
on a cousu
nous avons cousu
nous avez cousu
ils/elles ont cousu

Imperfect
je cousais
tu cousais
il/elle cousait
on cousait
nous cousions
vous cousiez
ils/elles cousaient

Simple past
je cousis
tu cousis
il/elle cousit
on cousit
nous cousîmes
vous cousîtes
ils/elles cousirent

Similar verbs

découdre   unpick
recoudre   sew up/back on again

Present participle	Past participle
cousant	cousu

Past perfect	Past anterior
j'avais cousu	j'eus cousu

Future	Future perfect
je coudrai	j'aurai cousu

Conditional	Conditional perfect
je coudrais	j'aurais cousu

Present subjunctive	Perfect subjunctive
que je couse	que j'aie cousu

Imperfect subjunctive	Pluperfect subjunctive
que je cousisse	que j'eusse cousu

Elle *a cousu* le bouton à la chemise.	She *sewed* the button on the shirt.
Tu pourrais me *recoudre* cet ourlet?	Could you *sew up* this seam *again* for me?
Elle *coud* une robe.	She's *making* a dress.
Elle *avait recousu* tout le devant de la jupe.	She *had resewn* all the front of the skirt.
Je *découdrais* tout ça, si j'avais le temps.	I'd *undo* all that stitching, if I had the time.

9g   Croire, *to believe*
Irregular -re verb

Imperative

crois! (tu)   croyez! (vous)   croyons! (nous)

Present
je crois
tu crois
il/elle croit
on croit
nous croyons
vous croyez
ils/elles croient

Perfect
j'ai cru
tu as cru
il/elle a cru
on a cru
nous avons cru
vous avez cru
ils/elles ont cru

Imperfect
je croyais
tu croyais
il/elle croyait
on croyait
nous croyions
vous croyiez
ils/elles croyaient

Simple past
je crus
tu crus
il/elle crut
on crut
nous crûmes
vous crûtes
ils/elles crurent

Notes

1. This is the only verb of this type.

Present participle	**Past participle**
croyant	cru
Past perfect	**Past anterior**
j'avais cru	j'eus cru
Future	**Future perfect**
je croirai	j'aurai cru
Conditional	**Conditional perfect**
je croirais	j'aurais cru
Present subjunctive	**Perfect subjunctive**
que je croie	que j'aie cru
que nous croyions	
Imperfect subjunctive	**Pluperfect subjunctive**
que je crusse	que j'eusse cru

– Tu *crois* qu'il arrivera bientôt?	– *Do* you *think* he'll arrive soon?
– Non, je ne *crois* pas.	– No, I *don't think* so.
Je *croyais* qu'il allait te prêter mille francs.	I thought he was going to lend you a thousand francs.
Croyez-vous en Dieu?	*Do* you *believe* in God?
Je n'*aurais* jamais *cru* . . .	I *would* never *have thought* . . .

9h Dire, *to say*
Irregular -re verb

Imperative

dis! (tu)	dites! (vous)	disons! (nous)

Present
je dis
tu dis
il/elle dit
on dit
nous disons
vous dites
ils/elles disent

Perfect
j'ai dit
tu as dit
il/elle a dit
on a dit
nous avons dit
vous avez dit
ils/elles ont dit

Imperfect
je disais
tu disais
il/elle disait
on disait
nous disions
vous disiez
ils/elles disaient

Simple past
je dis
tu dis
il/elle dit
on dit
nous dîmes
vous dîtes
ils/elles dirent

Similar verbs

contredire	contradict
interdire	forbid; prohibit
frire	fry
prédire	foretell, predict

Notes

1. Note similarities and differences between **dire**, **écrire**, **lire**.
2. **Suffire** (be sufficient) is conjugated like **dire**, except that the present indicative tense is **vous suffisez**, and the past participle is **suffi**.
3. **Frire** (fry) is found mainly in the past participle, **frit** (fried), and in the expression **faire frire** (fry food).

Que *dis*-tu?	What *do* you *say?*
	What *are* you *saying?*
Je lui *ai dit* de venir me voir.	I *told* him to come and see me.
***Dites*-lui bonjour de ma part.**	*Say* hello to her from me.

Present participle	Past participle
disant	dit

Past perfect	Past anterior
j'avais dit	j'eus dit

Future	Future perfect
je dirai	j'aurai dit

Conditional	Conditional perfect
je dirais	j'aurais dit

Present subjunctive	Perfect subjunctive
que je dise	que j'aie dit

Imperfect subjunctive	Pluperfect subjunctive
que je disse	que j'eusse dit

Il n'a rien dit.

He didn't *say* a thing.
(He *said* nothing.)

– **On se voit à quelle heure?**
– **Disons cinq heures.**

– What time shall we meet?
– *Let's say* five.

Et je dirais même plus . . .

And I'*d even go so far as to say* . . .

Louis X (dit le Hutin)

Louis X (*called* "the Quarrelsome")

Il n'y a plus rien à dire.

There's nothing more *to say.*

Comment dit-on en français . . ?

How do you *say* in French . . ?

Cela te dit d'aller au cinéma?

Do you *feel like* going to the movies?

– **Ça te dit quelque chose, cette adresse?**
– **Non, ça ne me dit rien.**

– Does that address *mean* anything to you?
– No, it doesn't *ring a bell.*

– **Veux-tu des pommes frites?**
– **Non, merci. Mon médecin me les a interdites.**

– Do you want some French fries?
– No, thanks. My doctor has forbidden me (to eat) them.

9i   Ecrire, *to write*
Irregular -re verb

Imperative

écris! (tu)   écrivez! (vous)   écrivons! (nous)

Present
j'écris
tu écris
il/elle écrit
on écrit
nous écrivons
vous écrivez
ils/elles écrivent

Perfect
j'ai écrit
tu as écrit
il/elle a écrit
on a écrit
nous avons écrit
vous avez écrit
ils/elles ont écrit

Imperfect
j'écrivais
tu écrivais
il/elle écrivait
on écrivait
nous écrivions
vous écriviez
ils/elles écrivaient

Simple past
j'écrivis
tu écrivis
il/elle écrivit
on écrivit
nous écrivîmes
nous écrivîtes
ils/elles écrivirent

Similar verbs

circonscrire	contain; confine
décrire	describe
inscrire	note down; write down
prescrire	prescribe; stipulate
proscrire	ban; prohibit
récrire	write down again
réinscrire	reinscribe; reregister
retranscrire	retranscribe
souscrire	subscribe
transcrire	copy out; transcribe; transliterate

Present participle écrivant	***Past participle*** écrit

Past perfect j'avais écrit	***Past anterior*** j'eus écrit
Future j'écrirai	***Future perfect*** j'aurai écrit
Conditional j'écrirais	***Conditional perfect*** j'aurais écrit
Present subjunctive que j'écrive	***Perfect subjunctive*** que j'aie écrit
Imperfect subjunctive que j'écrivisse	***Pluperfect subjunctive*** que j'eusse écrit

***Écris*-moi vite.**	*Write* soon.
Je lui *ai écrit* la semaine dernière.	I *wrote* to him last week.
Il faut que j'*écrive* une lettre.	I *must write* a letter.
***Décrivez* les voleurs.**	*Describe* the thieves.
Ne pas dépasser la dose prescrite.	Do not exceed the *recommended* dose.

9j   Faire, *to do, make*
Irregular -re verb

Imperative
fais! (tu)   faites! (vous)   faisons! (nous)

Present	Perfect
je fais	j'ai fait
tu fais	tu as fait
il/elle fait	il/elle a fait
on fait	on a fait
nous faisons	nous avons fait
vous faites	vous avez fait
ils/elles font	ils/elles ont fait

Imperfect	Simple past
je faisais	je fis
tu faisais	tu fis
il/elle faisait	il/elle fit
on faisait	on fit
nous faisions	nous fîmes
vous faisiez	vous fîtes
ils/elles faisaient	ils/elles firent

Similar verbs

contrefaire	imitate, mimic
défaire	dismantle
redéfaire	undo, take off, unpick again
refaire	redo
satisfaire	satisfy
surfaire	overrate, overprice

Que *fais*-tu?	What *are* you *doing?*
Je *fais* mes devoirs.	I'*m doing* my homework.
Il *fait* la vaisselle tous les jours.	He *does* the dishwashing every day.
J'aime *faire du cheval*.	I like *horseback-riding*.
***Faites* le plein!**	*Fill* up the tank!

Present participle	*Past participle*
faisant	fait

Past perfect	*Past anterior*
j'avais fait	j'eus fait
Future	*Future perfect*
je ferai	j'aurai fait
Conditional	*Conditional perfect*
je ferais	j'aurais fait
Present subjunctive	*Perfect subjunctive*
que je fasse	que j'aie fait
Imperfect subjunctive	*Pluperfect subjunctive*
que je fisse	que j'eusse fait

Il *fait* chaud.	It's hot (weather).
Quel temps *a*-t-il *fait* hier?	What *was* the weather like yesterday?
Tous les matins, on *faisait* une promenade ensemble.	Every morning we *used to* go for a walk together.
Que *feriez*-vous si votre père vendait la maison?	What *would you do* if your father sold the house?
Qu'est-ce tu *aurais fait* si je n'étais pas arrivé?	What *would* you *have done* if I hadn't arrived?
Je vais *faire du ski*.	I'm going *skiing*.
Que veux-tu que je *fasse*?	What do you want me to *do*?
Cela te *fera* du bien.	That *will do* you *good*.

9k Lire, *to read*
Irregular -re verb

Imperative
lis! (tu)   lisez! (vous)   lisons! (nous)

Present
je lis
tu lis
il/elle lit
on lit
nous lisons
vous lisez
ils/elles lisent

Perfect
j'ai lu
tu as lu
il/elle a lu
on a lu
nous avons lu
vous avez lu
ils/elles ont lu

Imperfect
je lisais
tu lisais
il/elle lisait
on lisait
nous lisions
vous lisiez
ils/elles lisaient

Simple past
je lus
tu lus
il/elle lut
on lut
nous lûmes
vous lûtes
ils/elles lurent

Similar verbs

élire   elect
réélire   reelect
relire   reread

Present participle	Past participle
lisant	lu

Past perfect	Past anterior
j'avais lu	j'eus lu

Future	Future perfect
je lirai	j'aurai lu

Conditional	Conditional perfect
je lirais	j'aurais lu

Present subjunctive	Perfect subjunctive
que je lise	que j'aie lu

Imperfect subjunctive	Pluperfect subjunctive
que je lusse	que j'eusse lu

Tu *as lu* le journal?	*Have* you *read* the paper?
Je *lis* beaucoup de romans policiers.	I *read* a lot of thrillers.
On l'*a élu* président.	He *was elected* president.
J'aimerais bien *relire* Le Rouge et le Noir.	I'd really like to *read* Le Rouge et le Noir *again*.
Lisez à haute voix . . .	*Read* aloud . . .
Tu sais *lire*?	Can you *read*?
Il alla prendre un abécédaire et je *lus* sans difficulté plusieurs pages. *La Gloire de mon père* (Marcel Pagnol)	He went and got an alphabet book and I *read* several pages without difficulty.

91   Mettre, *to put*
Irregular -re verb

Imperative
mets! (tu)   mettez! (vous)   mettons! (nous)

Present
je *mets*
tu *mets*
il/elle *met*
on *met*
nous mettons
vous mettez
ils/elles mettent

Perfect
j'ai *mis*
tu as *mis*
il/elle a *mis*
on a *mis*
nous avons *mis*
vous avez *mis*
ils/elles ont *mis*

Imperfect
je mettais
tu mettais
il/elle mettait
on mettait
nous mettions
vous mettiez
ils/elles mettaient

Simple past
je *mis*
tu *mis*
il/elle *mit*
on *mit*
nous *mîmes*
vous *mîtes*
ils/elles *mirent*

Similar verbs

admettre	admit	**permettre**	allow
commettre	commit	**promettre**	promise
compromettre	compromise	**réadmettre**	readmit
démettre	dislocate	**remettre**	put again
émettre	give/send out; emit	**retransmettre**	transmit again
entremettre (s')	mediate; intervene	**soumettre**	subject; subjugate
omettre	omit	**transmettre**	transmit

Notes

1. Italicized forms show differences from model verb **vendre** (➤9a).
2. **Battre** (to beat) and its compounds **combattre** (to combat), **abattre** (to slaughter; to dishearten) and others are conjugated exactly as **mettre** in all forms but the past participle, which is **battu (combattu, abattu)**.

Present participle	Past participle
mettant	*mis*

Past Perfect	Past anterior
j'avais *mis*	j'eus *mis*

Future	Future perfect
je mettrai	j'aurai *mis*

Conditional	Conditional perfect
je mettrais	j'aurais *mis*

Present subjunctive	Perfect subjunctive
que je *mette*	que j'aie *mis*

Imperfect subjunctive	Pluperfect subjunctive
que je *misse*	que j'eusse *mis*

Mettez-vous à ma place!	*Put* yourself in my position!
Où *as*-tu *mis* les billets?	Where *did* you *put* the tickets?
Je te *promets* qu'on ira à Paris.	I *promise* you we'll go to Paris.
Il ne veut rien *admettre.*	He won't *admit* a thing.
On ne me *permet* pas de sortir après neuf heures.	I'm not *allowed* to go out after nine.
On ne lui *permet* pas de sortir le soir.	They don't *allow* her to go out in the evening.
Je lui *ai permis* de m'accompagner.	I *allowed* him to go with me.
Va *mettre* la table!	Go and *lay* the table!
On *se bat!*	They'*re fighting!*

9m   Moudre, *to grind*
Irregular -re verb

Imperative
mouds! (tu)   moulez! (vous)   moulons! (nous)

Present	**Perfect**
je mouds	j'ai moulu
tu mouds	tu as moulu
il/elle moud	il/elle a moulu
on moud	on a moulu
nous moulons	nous avons moulu
vous moulez	vous avez moulu
ils/elles moulent	ils/elles ont moulu

Imperfect	**Simple past**
je moulais	je moulus
tu moulais	tu moulus
il/elle moulait	il/elle moulut
on moulait	on moulut
nous moulions	nous moulûmes
vous mouliez	vous moulûtes
ils/elles moulaient	ils/elles moulurent

Similar verbs

émoudre   sharpen; grind
remoudre   grind again

Notes

1. The forms are very similar to those of **coudre**, the intervening consonant being **-l-** in **moudre** (**-s-** in **coudre**).

Present participle	**Past participle**
moulant	moulu

Past perfect	**Past anterior**
j'avais moulu	j'eus moulu
Future	**Future perfect**
je moudrai	j'aurai moulu
Conditional	**Conditional perfect**
je moudrais	j'aurais moulu
Present subjunctive	**Perfect subjunctive**
que je moule	que j'aie moulu
Imperfect subjunctive	**Pluperfect subjunctive**
que je moulusse	que j'eusse moulu

Je vais *moudre* du café.	I'm going *to grind* some coffee.
On l'*a moulu* de coups.	They *beat* him up.
Elle *moulait* du café pour ses invités.	She *was grinding* some coffee for her guests.
Il a dit qu'*il moudrait* du café pour ce soir.	He said he *would grind* some coffee for this evening.
Je *mouds* un peu de poivre.	I'*m grinding* a little pepper.

9n   Naître, *to be born*
Irregular -re verb

Imperative
nais! (tu)   naissez! (vous)   naissons! (nous)

Present	**Perfect**
je nais	je suis né(-e)
tu nais	tu es né(-e)
il/elle naît	il est né
on naît	elle est née
nous naissons	on est né
vous naissez	nous sommes nés/nées
ils/elles naissent	vous êtes né/née/nés/nées
	ils sont nés
	elles sont nées

Imperfect	**Simple past**
je naissais	je naquis
tu naissais	tu naquis
il/elle naissait	il/elle naquit
on naissait	on naquit
nous naissions	nous naquîmes
vous naissiez	vous naquîtes
ils/elles naissaient	ils/elles naquirent

Similar verbs

renaître   be born again; reborn, revived;
                                     spring up again

Notes

1. This verb is not often found in the present or imperfect tenses; it appears most often found are the perfect and simple past forms.
2. It is conjugated with **être** in compound tenses.

Present participle	Past participle
naissant	né

Past perfect	Past anterior
j'étais né(-e)	je fus né(-e)

Future	Future perfect
je naîtrai	je serai né(-e)

Conditional	Conditional perfect
je naîtrais	je serais né(-e)

Present subjunctive	Perfect subjunctive
que je naisse	que je sois né(-e)

Imperfect subjunctive	Pluperfect subjunctive
que je naquisse	que je fusse né(-e)

– Quel est votre lieu de naissance?	– What is your place of birth?
– Je suis né à Marseille.	– I was born in Marseille.
Il est né, le divin enfant . . . (French traditional carol)	He is born, the divine child . . .
Je ne savais pas qu'il était né en Corse.	I didn't know he was born in Corsica.
Tous nos enfants sont nés au Canada.	All our children were born in Canada.

9o   **Peindre**, *to paint*
Irregular -re verb ending in -indre

Imperative
peins! (tu)   peignez! (vous)   peignons! (nous)

Present
je peins
tu peins
il/elle peint
on peint
nous peignons
vous peignez
ils/elles peignent

Perfect
j'ai peint
tu as peint
il/elle a peint
on a peint
nous avons peint
vous avez peint
ils/elles ont peint

Imperfect
je peignais
tu peignais
il/elle peignait
on peignait
nous peignions
vous peigniez
ils/elles peignaient

Simple past
je peignis
tu peignis
il/elle/on peignit
on peignit
nous peignîmes
vous peignîtes
ils/elles peignirent

Similar verbs

craindre	fear
dépeindre	depict
éteindre	extinguish, put out
étreindre	embrace, hug
plaindre	pity
(re)joindre	join (again)
repeindre	repaint

Notes

1. **Se plaindre** (to complain), a reflexive verb (conjugated with **être** in compound tenses), follows the same pattern.
2. **Craindre** and **plaindre** take **craint** and **plaint** as their past participles.
3. **Rejoindre** takes **rejoint** as its past participle.

Present participle	**Past participle**
peignant	peint

Past perfect	**Past anterior**
j'avais peint	j'eus peint
Future	**Future perfect**
je peindrai	j'aurai peint
Conditional	**Conditional perfect**
je peindrais	j'aurais peint
Present subjunctive	**Perfect subjunctive**
que je peigne	j'aie peint
Imperfect subjunctive	**Pluperfect subjunctive**
que je peignisse	que j'eusse peint

Franchement, je le *plains*.	Quite honestly, I *feel sorry for* him.
De quoi te *plains*-tu?	What are you *complaining* about?
J'*ai repeint* l'appartement.	I'*ve repainted* the apartment.
Monet *peignait* très souvent sa femme.	Monet often *painted* his wife.
Elle a eteint sa cigarette.	She put out her cigarette.
"Pour faire le portrait d'un oiseau *peindre* d'abord une cage avec une porte ouverte." *Paroles* (Jacques Prévert)	"To paint a portrait of a bird, first *paint* a cage with an open door."
Nous nous *sommes rejoints* à Nice.	We *rejoined each other* in Nice.
Que *craignez vous*?	What *are you afraid of*?

9p Plaire, *to please*
Irregular -re verb

Imperative
plais! (tu)   plaisez! (vous)   plaisons! (nous)

Present
je plais
tu plais
il/elle plaît
on plaît
nous plaisons
vous plaisez
ils/elles plaisent

Perfect
j'ai plu
tu as plu
il/elle a plu
on a plu
nous avons plu
vous avez plu
ils ont plu

Imperfect
je plaisais
tu plaisais
il/elle plaisait
on plaisait
nous plaisions
vous plaisiez
ils/elles plaisaient

Simple past
je plus
tu plus
il/elle plut
on plut
nous plûmes
vous plûtes
ils/elles plurent

Similar verbs

déplaire   displease
taire   be silent

Notes

    1. **Taire** has no accent on the third-person singular present tense: **il se tait**.

Present participle	*Past participle*
plaisant	plu

Past perfect	*Past anterior*
j'avais plu	j'eus plu
Future	*Future perfect*
je plairai	j'aurai plu
Conditional	*Conditional perfect*
je plairais	j'aurais plu
Present subjunctive	*Perfect subjunctive*
que je plaise	que j'aie plu
Imperfect subjunctive	*Pluperfect subjunctive*
que je plusse	que j'eusse plu

S'il vous *plaît.*	*Please.*
Il me *plaît* beaucoup.	I *like* him alot. (*Literally, "He pleases me,"*)
*Taisez-*vous, les enfants.	*Be quiet*, children.
Ils *se sont tus.*	They *fell silent.*
Ça me *plairait* beaucoup que tu viennes.	I'*d* really *like* you to come.
J'ai essayé de lui *plaire.*	I *tried* to please her.

9q   Prendre, *to take*
Irregular -re verb

Imperative
prends! (tu)   prenez! (vous)   prenons! (nous)

Present	Perfect
je prends	j'ai pris
tu prends	tu as pris
il/elle prend	il/elle a pris
on prend	on a pris
nous prenons	nous avons pris
vous prenez	vous avez pris
ils/elles prennent	ils/elles ont pris

Imperfect	Simple past
je prenais	je pris
tu prenais	tu pris
il/elle prenait	il/elle prit
on prenait	on prit
nous prenions	nous prîmes
vous preniez	vous prîtes
ils/elles prenaient	ils/elles prirent

Similar verbs

apprendre	learn	**entreprendre**	begin; undertake
(s')éprendre	fall in love		embark upon
comprendre	understand;	**réapprendre**	relearn
	consist of	**reprendre**	resume; recapture
		surprendre	surprise

Qu'est-ce que tu *prends*?	What are you *having* (to drink)?
J'ai toujours mal à la tête, mais j'*ai pris* des comprimés.	I have still got a headache, but I'*ve taken* some tablets.
Où *as*-tu *appris* à nager?	Where *did* you *learn* to swim?

Present participle	**Past participle**
prenant	pris

Past perfect
j'avais pris

Past anterior
j'eus pris

Future
je prendrai

Future perfect
j'aurai pris

Conditional
je prendrais

Conditional perfect
j'aurais pris

Present subjunctive
que je prenne
que tu prennes
qu'il/elle prenne
qu'on prenne
que nous prenions
que vous preniez
qu'ils/elles prennent

Perfect subjunctive
que j'aie pris

Imperfect subjunctive
que je prisse

Pluperfect subjunctive
que j'eusse pris

Tu veux un biscuit?
Prends-en deux!

Do you want a biscuit?
Take two!

J'aime ce pull
— je le *prends*.

I like this sweater
— I'll *take* it.

Cela lui *apprendra* à vivre.

That *will teach* him a lesson.

Le service n'est pas *compris*.

Service is not *included*.

Quand il parle anglais,
personne ne le *comprend*.

When he speaks English,
no one *understands* him.

Je n'*ai* rien *compris*
— comment veux-tu que je
comprenne?

I *didn't understand* a thing
— how to you expect me to
understand?

9r Résoudre, *to resolve*
Irregular -re verb

Imperative

résous! (tu)	résolvez! (vous)	résolvons! (nous)

Present
je résous
tu résous
il/elle résout
on résout
nous résolvons
vous résolvez
ils/elles résolvent

Perfect
j'ai résolu
tu as résolu
il/elle a résolu
on a résolu
nous avons résolu
vous avez résolu
ils/elles ont résolu

Imperfect
je résolvais
tu résolvais
il/elle résolvait
on résolvait
nous résolvions
vous résolviez
ils/elles résolvaient

Simple past
je résolus
tu résolus
il/elle résolut
on résolut
nous résolûmes
vous résolûtes
ils/elles résolurent

Similar verbs

absoudre   absolve; pardon
dissoudre   dissolve

Present participle	**Past participle**
résolvant	résolu

Past perfect	**Past anterior**
j'avais résolu	j'eus résolu
Future	**Future perfect**
je résoudrai	j'aurai résolu
Conditional	**Conditional perfect**
je résoudrais	j'aurais résolu
Present subjunctive	**Perfect subjunctive**
que je résolve	que j'aie résolu
Imperfect subjunctive	**Pluperfect subjunctive**
que je résolusse	que j'eusse résolu

Il n'*a* pas *résolu* le problème.	He *has*n't *solved* the problem.
Je *me suis résolu* à quitter la compagnie.	I *made up my mind* to leave the company.
Il faut faire *dissoudre* le sel dans de l'eau.	You have to *dissolve* the salt in water.
Elle *a résolu* de partir.	She'*s made up her mind* to leave.
Je vous *absous!*	I *forgive* you!

9s   Rire, *to laugh*
Irregular -re verb

Imperative
ris! (tu)   riez! (vous)   rions! (nous)

Present	**Perfect**
je ris	j'ai ri
tu ris	tu as ri
il/elle rit	il/elle a ri
on rit	on a ri
nous rions	nous avons ri
vous riez	vous avez ri
ils/elles rient	ils ont ri

Imperfect	**Simple past**
je riais	je ris
tu riais	tu ris
il/elle riait	il/elle rit
on riait	on rit
nous riions	nous rîmes
vous riiez	vous rîtes
ils/elles riaient	ils/elles rirent

Similar verbs

sourire   smile

Present participle	*Past participle*
riant	ri

Past perfect	*Past anterior*
j'avais ri	j'eus ri
Future	*Future perfect*
je rirai	j'aurai ri
Conditional	*Conditional perfect*
je rirais	j'aurais ri
Present subjunctive	*Perfect subjunctive*
que je rie	que j'aie ri
Imperfect subjunctive	*Pluperfect subjunctive*
que je risse	que j'eusse ri

"Tu *souriais*, **et moi je *souriais* de même."** Barbara (Jacques Prévert)	"You *were smiling*, and I *smiled* too"
***Rira* bien qui *rira* le dernier.**	He who *laughs* last *laughs* best.
Ne *riez* pas.	Don't *laugh*.
On s'est tordu de *rire*.	We cracked up laughing.
On *a* bien *ri*.	We *had* a good *laugh*.
Elle *riait* de lui.	She *was laughing* at him.
Tu *ris* — pourquoi?	You're *laughing* — why?
Ils *rient* aux éclats!	They're *roaring with laughter*!

9t soustraire, *to subtract*
Irregular -re verb

Imperative
soustrais! (tu)   soustrayez! (vous)   soustrayons! (nous)

Present
je soustrais
tu soustrais
il/elle soustrait
on soustrait
nous soustrayons
vous soustrayez
ils/elles soustraient

Perfect
j'ai soustrait
tu as soustrait
il/elle a soustrait
on a soustrait
nous avons soustrait
vous avez soustrait
ils/elles ont soustrait

Imperfect
je soustrayais
tu soustrayais
il/elle soustrayait
on soustrayait
nous soustrayions
vous soustrayiez
ils/elles soustrayaient

Simple past
—

Similar verbs

abstraire   abstract
distraire   entertain; divert
extraire   extract

Present participle	***Past participle***
soustrayant	soustrait

Past perfect	***Past anterior***
j'avais soustrait	j'eus soustrait
Future	***Future perfect***
je soustrairai	j'aurai soustrait
Conditional	***Conditional perfect***
je soustrairais	j'aurais soustrait
Present subjunctive	***Perfect subjunctive***
que je soustraie	que j'aie soustrait
Imperfect subjunctive	***Pluperfect subjunctive***
—	que j'eusse soustrait

On *trait* les vaches à cinq heures.	We *milk* the cows at five o'clock.
J'aime regarder la télé pour me *distraire*.	I like watching TV for *entertainment*.
On *extrait* le charbon ici.	They *mine* coal here.
Dans le passé on *extrayait* le marbre.	In the past they *quarried* marble.
Tu m'*as distrait*.	You *distracted* me.
***Soustrayez* dix dollars de notre compte.**	*Subtract* ten dollars from our bill.

9u   Suivre, *to follow*
Irregular -re verb

Imperative
suis! (tu)   suivez! (vous)   suivons! (nous)

Present	**Perfect**
je suis	j'ai suivi
tu suis	tu as suivi
il/elle suit	il/elle a suivi
on suit	on a suivi
nous suivons	nous avons suivi
vous suivez	vous avez suivi
ils/elles suivent	ils/elles ont suivi

Imperfect	**Simple past**
je suivais	je suivis
tu suivais	tu suivis
il/elle suivait	il/elle suivit
on suivait	on suivit
nous suivions	nous suivîmes
vous suiviez	vous suivîtes
ils/elles suivaient	ils/elles suivirent

Similar verbs

poursuivre   pursue

Notes

1. **S'ensuivre** (to result, ensue) is also conjugated this way (using **être** in compound tenses).
2. There is rarely confusion between the two meanings of **je suis** (I am/I follow); the context normally makes the sense clear.

Present participle	**Past participle**
suivant	suivi

Past perfect	**Past anterior**
j'avais suivi	j'eus suivi
Future	**Future perfect**
je suivrai	j'aurai suivi
Conditional	**Conditional perfect**
je suivrais	j'aurais suivi
Present subjunctive	**Perfect subjunctive**
que je suive	que j'aie suivi
Imperfect subjunctive	**Pluperfect subjunctive**
que je suivisse	que j'eusse suivi

Suivez-moi, s'il vous plaît!	*Follow* me, please.
Ce chien nous *suit* depuis une heure.	This dog *has been following* us for an hour.
La police *a poursuivi* les voleurs.	The police *pursued* the thieves
A suivre.	*To be continued.*
Il *a été poursuivi* en justice.	He *was prosecuted.*

9v   Vaincre, *to defeat*
Irregular -re verb

Imperative

vaincs! (tu)   vainquez! (vous)   vainquons! (nous)

Present	**Perfect**
je vaincs	j'ai vaincu
tu vaincs	tu as vaincu
il/elle vainc	il/elle a vaincu
on vainc	on a vaincu
nous vainquons	nous avons vaincu
vous vainquez	vous avez vaincu
ils/elles vainquent	ils/elles ont vaincu

Imperfect	**Simple past**
je vainquais	je vainquis
tu vainquais	tu vainquis
il/elle vainquait	il/elle vainquit
on vainquait	on vainquit
nous vainquions	nous vainquîmes
vous vainquiez	vous vainquîtes
ils/elles vainquaient	ils/elles vainquirent

Similar verbs

convaincre   convince

Notes

1. In front of a vowel (except **-u-**) the **-c-** of **vaincre** changes to **-qu-**.

Present participle	Past participle
vainquant	vaincu

Past perfect	Past anterior
j'avais vaincu	j'eus vaincu

Future	Future perfect
je vaincrai	j'aurai vaincu

Conditional	Conditional perfect
je vaincrais	j'aurais vaincu

Present subjunctive	Perfect subjunctive
que je vainque	que j'aie vaincu

Imperfect subjunctive	Pluperfect subjunctive
que je vainquisse	que j'eusse vaincu

Il m'*a convaincu* d'abandonner le projet.	He *convinced* me to give up the project.
Nous *avons vaincu!*	We *won!*
Je ne *suis* pas *convaincu.*	I'*m* not *convinced.*
Nous *vaincrons!*	We *shall win!*
Il *va vaincre* la maladie.	He *will overcome* the illness.
Il *était vaincu* d'avance.	He *was defeated* before he started.
Wellington *vainquit* à Waterloo.	Wellington *won* at Waterloo.

9w   Vivre, *to live*
Irregular -re verb

Imperative

vis! (tu)   vivez! (vous)   vivons! (nous)

Present
je vis
tu vis
il/elle vit
on vit
nous vivons
vous vivez
ils/elles vivent

Perfect
j'ai vécu
tu as vécu
il/elle a vécu
on a vécu
nous avons vécu
vous avez vécu
ils/elles ont vécu

Imperfect
je vivais
tu vivais
il/elle vivait
on vivait
nous vivions
vous viviez
ils/elles vivaient

Simple past
je vécus
tu vécus
il/elle vécut
on vécut
nous vécûmes
vous vécûtes
ils/elles vécurent

Similar verbs

revivre   live again
survivre   survive

Present participle	Past participle
vivant	vécu

Past perfect	Past anterior
j'avais vécu	j'eus vécu
Future	**Future perfect**
je vivrai	j'aurai vécu
Conditional	**Conditional perfect**
je vivrais	j'aurais vécu
Present subjunctive	**Perfect subjunctive**
que je vive	que j'aie vécu
Imperfect subjunctive	**Pluperfect subjunctive**
que je vécusse	que j'eusse vécu

Tant que je *vivrai* . . .	As long as I *live* . . .
Il *a vécu* à Rome.	He *lived* in Rome.
En 1883, Gauguin *vivait* à Paris	In 1883, Gauguin *was living* in Paris.
On a juste de quoi *vivre*.	We have just enough *to live* on.
Nous *vivons* chez nos parents.	We *live* at our parents' house.
Pétrarque *vécut* en Provence.	Petrarch *lived* in Provence.
Ils n'*avaient* jamais *vécu* à Paris.	They *had* never *lived* in Paris.
Je ne crois pas qu'il sur*vive* très longtemps.	I don't think he'*ll survive* for long.

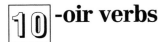 **-oir verbs**

10a   s'asseoir, *to sit down*

Irregular reflexive verb in -oir

Imperative

assieds-toi! (tu)   asseyez-vous! (vous)   asseyons-nous (nous)

Present

je m'assieds (m'assois)
tu t'assieds (t'assois)
il/elle s'assied (s'assoit)
on s'assied (s'assoit)
nous nous asseyons
vous vous asseyez
ils/elles s'asseyent (assoient)

Perfect

je me suis assis(-e)
tu t'es assis(-e)
il s'est assis
elle s'est assise
on s'est assis
nous nous sommes assis(-es)
vous vous êtes assis(-e)(-es)
ils se sont assis
elles se sont assises

Imperfect

je m'asseyais
tu t'asseyais
il/elle s'asseyait
on s'asseyait
nous nous asseyions
vous vous asseyiez
ils/elles s'asseyaient

Simple past

je m'assis
tu t'assis
il/elle s'assit
on s'assit
nous nous assîmes
vous vous assîtes
ils/elles s'assirent

Notes

1. This verb is the only one of its kind. Where two forms exist, the first is more common; those with **-oi-** are much less common.

Present participle	**Past participle**
asseyant/assoyant	assis

Past perfect
je m'étais assis(-e)

Past anterior
je me fus assis(-e)

Future
je m'asseyerai or
je m'assiérai

Future perfect
je me serai assis(-e)

Conditional
je m'asseyerais or
je m'assoirais

Conditional perfect
je me serais assis(-e)

Present subjunctive
que je m'asseye   or
que je m'assoie

Perfect subjunctive
que je me sois assis(-e)

Imperfect subjunctive
que je m'assisse

Pluperfect subjunctive
que je me fusse assis(-e)

Asseyons-nous devant le feu, où il fait chaud.
Lets sit down in front of the fire, where it's warm.

Asseyez-vous, les enfants.
Sit down, children.

Je *me suis assis* devant lui.
I *sat down* in front of him.

Où voulez-vous *vous asseoir?*
Where do you want to *sit?*

10b Devoir, *to have to*
Irregular modal verb in -oir

Imperative

dois! (tu)   devez! (vous)   devons! (nous)

Present
je dois
tu dois
il/elle doit
on doit
nous devons
vous devez
ils/elles doivent

Perfect
j'ai dû
tu as dû
il/elle a dû
on a dû
nous avons dû
vous avez dû
ils/elles ont dû

Imperfect
je devais
tu devais
il/elle devait
on devait
nous devions
vous deviez
ils/elles devaient

Simple past
je dus
tu dus
il/elle dut
on dut
nous dûmes
vous dûtes
ils/elles durent

Notes

1. The imperative is rarely found.
2. If the past participle requires a feminine agreement, the spelling is **due.**
3. As a full verb, **devoir** means "to owe."
4. It is the only verb of its type, though similarities with **pouvoir** and **vouloir** will be obvious (➤10e, 10k).

Examples of use as a full verb

Je lui *dois* cinquante francs.	I *owe* her fifty francs.
Il me *devait* un million de francs.	He *owed* me a million francs

Present participle	**Past participle**
devant	dû

Past perfect	**Past anterior**
j'avais dû	j'eus dû
Future	**Future perfect**
je devrai	j'aurai dû
Conditional	**Conditional perfect**
je devrais	j'aurais dû
Present subjunctive	**Perfect subjunctive**
que je doive	que j'aie dû
Imperfect subjunctive	**Pluperfect subjunctive**
que je dusse	que j'eusse dû

Examples of use as a modal verb

Tu *dois* y arriver avant huit heures.	You *must* get there by eight o'clock.
On *doit* écouter les instructions.	We *must* listen to the instructions.
On *devra* partir à l'aube.	We'*ll have to* leave at dawn.
Il *a dû* travailler jusqu'à minuit.	He *had to* work until midnight.
Il *a dû* avoir un accident.	He *must have* had an accident.
Elle *devait* l'accompagner en vacances.	She *was supposed* to go on vacation with him.
On *devrait* téléphoner tout de suite.	Someone *ought to* phone immediately.
Tu *aurais dû* lui offrir des fleurs.	You *ought to have* given her some flowers.

10c   Falloir, *to have to*
Irregular impersonal modal verb in -oir

Imperative

—

Present	**Perfect**
il faut	il a fallu

Imperfect	**Simple past**
il fallait	il fallut

Notes

1. This verb only exists in the third-person singular, and covers meanings from "it is necessary," "one must", to "we have to", "you have to."
2. **Il me faut** means "I need." (The addition of the personal indirect object pronoun personalizes the meaning.)

Il *faut* appeler les pompiers.	We *have to* call the fire department.
Il *faut* arriver à l'heure.	You *must* arrive on time.
Il *faut* que je voie mes cousins.	I *must* see my cousins.
Il *a fallu* nettoyer la maison.	We *had to* clean the house (and we did).
Il *faudrait* acheter du pain.	We *ought to* buy some bread.

Present participle	Past participle
—	fallu

Past perfect	Past anterior
il avait fallu	il eut fallu

Future	Future perfect
il faudra	il aura fallu

Conditional	Conditional perfect
il faudrait	il aurait fallu

Present subjunctive	Perfect subjunctive
qu'il faille	qu'il ait fallu

Imperfect subjunctive	Pluperfect subjunctive
qu'il fallût	qu'il eut fallu

Si Dieu n'existait pas, il **_faudrait_ l'inventer.** (Voltaire)	If God did not exist, we _would have_ to invent him.
Il me _faut_ des oeufs.	I _need_ some eggs.
Il ne _faut_ pas courir!	We don't _need_ to run!
Il ne _faut_ jamais nager seul.	You _should_ never swim alone.
Il _aurait fallu_ téléphoner plus tôt.	Someone _ought to have_ phoned earlier.
Il _fallut_ signer l'Armistice en juin 1940.	It _was necessary_ to sign the Armistice in June 1940.

10d   Pleuvoir, *to rain*
Irregular impersonal verb in -oir

Imperative
—

Present	**Perfect**
il pleut	il a plu

Imperfect	**Simple past**
il pleuvait	il plut

Notes

1. This impersonal verb is normally only found in the third-person singular. Occasionally a figurative usage may give rise to a plural verb. Example: **Les coups de fusil pleuvent sur les hommes**, "Gunfire rained down on the men."
2. There are no other verbs like it.

Present participle	*Past participle*
pleuvant	plu

Past perfect	**Past anterior**
il avait plu	il eut plu

Future	**Future perfect**
il pleuvra	il aura plu

Conditional	**Conditional perfect**
il pleuvrait	il aurait plu

Present subjunctive	**Perfect subjunctive**
qu'il pleuve	qu'il ait plu

Imperfect subjunctive	**Pluperfect subjunctive**
qu'il plût	qu'il eût plu

Il *pleut*.	It's *raining*.
Il va *pleuvoir*.	It's going *to rain*.
Il a *plu* hier.	It *rained* yesterday.
J'espère qu'il ne *pleuvra* pas au mois de juillet.	I hope it *won't rain* in July.
Il *pleuvait* toute la journée.	It *was raining* all day long.
Il a dit qu'il *pleuvrait*.	He said it *would rain*.
Elle m'a dit qu'il *avait plu* longtemps.	She told me it *had rained* for a long time.

10e   Pouvoir, *to be able*
Irregular modal verb in -oir

Imperative
—

Present	**Perfect**
je peux/je puis	j'ai pu
tu peux	tu as pu
il/elle peut	il/elle a pu
on peut	on a pu
nous pouvons	nous avons pu
vous pouvez	vous avez pu
ils/elles peuvent	ils/elles ont pu

Imperfect	**Simple past**
je pouvais	je pus
tu pouvais	tu pus
il/elle pouvait	il/elle put
on pouvait	on put
nous pouvions	nous pûmes
vous pouviez	vous pûtes
ils/elles pouvaient	ils/elles purent

Notes

1. There are no other verbs like **pouvoir**, though similarities with **devoir** and **vouloir** will be evident (➤10b, 10k, respectively).
2. The various tenses of **pouvoir** convey a full variety of meanings.
3. **Puis-je?** "May I?" is going out of use and is often considered old-fashioned.

Present participle	**Past participle**
pouvant	pu

Past perfect	**Past anterior**
j'avais pu	j'eus pu

Future	**Future perfect**
je pourrai	j'aurai pu

Conditional	**Conditional perfect**
je pourrais	j'aurais pu

Present subjunctive	**Perfect subjunctive**
que je puisse	que j'aie pu
que nous puissions	

Imperfect subjunctive	**Pluperfect subjunctive**
que je pusse	que j'eusse pu

Je *peux* entrer?	*May* I come in?
Il ne *peut* pas fermer cette fenêtre.	He *can*'t close that window.
On *peut* aller à la patinoire.	We *can* go to the skating-rink.
On *pourra* y aller en voiture.	We'*ll be able to* go there by car.
Il *pourrait* pleuvoir plus tard.	It *might* rain later.
Pourriez-vous me passer le sel?	*Could* you pass me the salt?
À l'époque on *pouvait* y acheter toutes sortes de choses.	At the time you *could* buy all sorts of things there.
Tu *aurais pu* me le dire!	You *could have* told me!
J'*ai pu* réparer la serrure.	I'*ve managed* to fix the lock.
Je regrette qu'on ne *puisse* plus y aller.	I'm sorry you *can*'t go there any more.

10f Promouvoir, *to promote, encourage*
Irregular verb in -oir

Imperative

promeus! (tu)	promouvez! (vous)	promouvons! (nous)

Present
je promeus
tu promeus
il/elle promeut
on promeut
nous promouvons
vous promouvez
ils/elles promeuvent

Perfect
j'ai promu
tu as promu
il/elle a promu
on a promu
nous avons promu
vous avez promu
ils/elles ont promu

Imperfect
je promouvais
tu promouvais
il/elle promouvait
on promouvait
nous promouvions
vous promouviez
ils promouvaient

Simple past
je promus
tu promus
il/elle promut
on promut
nous promûmes
vous promûtes
ils promurent

Similar verbs

émouvoir	affect; disturb; arouse
mouvoir	move

Notes

1. **Promouvoir** is found most frequently in the infinitive and compound tenses.

Present participle	**Past participle**
promouvant	promu

Past perfect	**Past anterior**
j'avais promu	j'eus promu

Future	**Future perfect**
je promouvrai	j'aurai promu

Conditional	**Conditional perfect**
je promouvrais	j'aurais promu

Present subjunctive	**Perfect subjunctive**
que je promeuve	que j'aie promu

Imperfect subjunctive	**Pluperfect subjunctive**
que je promusse	que j'eusse promu

On m'*a promu*.	I'*ve* been *promoted*.
Il faut *promouvoir* l'étude des langues vivantes.	It's necessary to *encourage* the study of modern languages.
Je *suis ému*.	I *am overcome* (*with emotion*).
Cette musique m'*a* toujours *ému*.	This music *has* always *moved* me.
La misère de ces pauvres gens l'*émouvait* profondément.	The poverty of those poor folk *moved* him deeply.
Les grèves de 1995 *émurent* profondément la population Française.	The strike in 1995 deeply *troubled* the French people.

10g   Recevoir, *to receive*
Irregular *-oir* verb ending in *-cevoir*

Imperative

reçois! (tu)	recevez! (vous)	recevons! (nous)

Present
je reçois
tu reçois
il/elle reçoit
on reçoit
nous recevons
vous recevez
ils/elles reçoivent

Perfect
j'ai reçu
tu as reçu
il/elle a reçu
on a reçu
nous avons reçu
vous avez reçu
ils/elles ont reçu

Imperfect
je recevais
tu recevais
il/elle recevait
on recevait
nous recevions
vous receviez
ils/elles recevaient

Simple past
je reçus
tu reçus
il/elle reçut
on reçut
nous reçûmes
vous reçûtes
ils/elles reçurent

Similar verbs

apercevoir	notice; see	**concevoir**	imagine; conceive
décevoir	deceive; disappoint	**percevoir**	perceive; detect; make out

Notes

1. As usual the cedilla is required whenever **c** precedes **o** or **u**.

Present participle	*Past participle*
recevant	reçu

Past perfect	*Past anterior*
j'avais reçu	j'eus reçu
Future	*Future perfect*
je recevrai	j'aurai reçu
Conditional	*Conditional perfect*
je recevrais	j'aurais reçu
Present subjunctive	*Perfect subjunctive*
que je reçoive	que j'aie reçu
qu'ils/elles reçoivent	
Imperfect subjunctive	*Pluperfect subjunctive*
que je reçusse	que j'eusse reçu

Le courier

– **Tous les matins, je *reçois* au moins trois factures.**

– **Qu'est-ce que vous *avez reçu* ce matin?**

– **Rien! Mais je n'*ai* pas encore *aperçu* le facteur.**

Tu *recevras* ma lettre demain.

Tu l'*aurais reçue* ce matin si je l'avais postée en ville.

On *a reçu* le maire.

D'ici on *aperçoit* le sommet de la montagne.

The mail

– Every morning I *receive* at least three bills.

– What *have* you *received* this morning?

– Nothing! But I *haven*'t yet *caught sight of* the mailman/postman.

You'*ll receive* my letter tomorrow.

You *would have received* it this morning if I'd posted it in town.

They *entertained* the mayor.

From here you *can* just *glimpse* the mountain top.

10h   Savoir, *to know*
Irregular modal verb in -oir

Imperative

sache! (tu)   sachez! (vous)   sachons! (nous)

Present	**Perfect**
je sais	j'ai su
tu sais	tu as su
il/elle sait	il/elle a su
on sait	on a su
nous savons	nous avons su
vous savez	vous avez su
ils/elles savent	ils/elles ont su

Imperfect	**Simple past**
je savais	je sus
tu savais	tu sus
il/elle savait	il/elle sut
on savait	on sut
nous savions	nous sûmes
vous saviez	vous sûtes
ils/elles savaient	ils/elles surent

Notes

1. This verb is important in two areas: (i) it is used for knowing a fact; (ii) it also has the meaning of "to be able," in the sense of having acquired a skill.
2. It should not be used for knowing people, countries, or works of art, music, theater, literature etc., where the correct verb is **connaître** (➤9e).

Examples of use as a full verb

– **Quelle heure est-il?**	– What time is it?
– **Je ne *sais* pas.**	– I *don't know*.
Je ne *savais* pas qu'il était à New York.	I *didn't know* he was in New York.
Je ne veux pas qu'on *sache* mon nom.	I don't want anyone to *know* my name.
Il *a su* son nom.	He *found out* her name.

148

Present participle	*Past participle*
sachant	su

Past perfect	*Past anterior*
j'avais su	j'eus su

Future	*Future perfect*
je saurai	j'aurai su

Conditional	*Conditional perfect*
je saurais	j'aurais su

Present subjunctive	*Perfect subjunctive*
que je sache	que j'aie su
que nous sachions	

Imperfect subjunctive	*Pluperfect subjunctive*
que je susse	que j'eusse su

Examples of use as a full verb

On ne *sait* jamais.	You never *know*.
Il *saura* les détails demain.	He'*ll know* the details tomorrow.
Finalement, on *sut* que Dreyfus était innocent.	In the end, people *learnt* that Dreyfus was innocent.
Il m'a dit qu'il n'*avait* pas *su* le numéro de la maison.	He told me he *had*n't *known* the house number.

Example of use as a modal verb

Je ne *saurais* pas le dire.	I *could*n't say.
Tu *sais* jouer du piano?	*Can* you play the piano?
Vous *savez* nager?	*Can* you swim?
A cette époque je ne *savais* pas jouer du violon.	At that time I *could*n't play the violin.

10i   Valoir, *to be worth*
Irregular verb in *-oir*

Imperative
vaux! (tu)   valez! (vous)   valons! (nous)

Present
je vaux
tu vaux
il/elle vaut
on vaut
nous valons
vous valez
ils/elles valent

Perfect
j'ai valu
tu as valu
il/elle a valu
on a valu
nous avons valu
vous avez valu
ils/elles ont valu

Imperfect
je valais
tu valais
il/elle valait
on valait
nous valions
vous valiez
ils/elles valaient

Simple past
je valus
tu valus
il/elle valut
on valut
nous valûmes
vous valûtes
ils/elles valurent

Similar verbs

équivaloir   be equivalent; amount to
prévaloir   prevail
revaloir   pay back

Notes

1. Impersonal usage: **il vaut mieux**, "it is better."

Present participle	Past participle
valant	valu

Past perfect	Past anterior
j'avais valu	j'eus valu

Future	Future perfect
ja vaudrai	j'aurai valu

Conditional	Conditional perfect
je vaudrais	j'aurais valu

Present subjunctive	Perfect subjunctive
que je vaille	que j'aie valu
que tu vailles	
qu'il/elle vaille	
qu'on vaille	
que nous valions	
que vous valiez	
qu'ils/elles vaillent	

Imperfect subjunctive	Pluperfect subjunctive
que je valusse	que j'eusse valu

Ça *vaut* combien?	How much is that *worth?*
Ce tableau *vaut* un million.	That painting is *worth* a million.
Ce film *vaut* la peine d'être vu.	That movie is *worth* seeing.
Ce type ne *vaut* pas cher.	That guy's not much *good.*
Ce café ne *vaut* pas le brésilien.	This coffee's not *as good* as the Brazilian.
Cette affaire lui *a valu* bien des soucis.	That matter *caused* him a lot of worry.
Il *vaut mieux* partir.	It'*s better* to leave.
Il *vaudrait mieux* partir tout de suite.	It *would be better* to leave at once.

10j   Voir, *to see*
Irregular verb in *-oir*

Imperative

vois! (tu)   voyez! (vous)   voyons! (nous)

Present	**Perfect**
je vois	j'ai vu
tu vois	tu as vu
il/elle voit	il/elle a vu
on voit	on a vu
nous voyons	nous avons vu
vous voyez	vous avez vu
ils voient	ils ont vu

Imperfect	**Simple past**
je voyais	je vis
tu voyais	tu vis
il/elle voyait	il/elle vit
on voyait	on vit
nous voyions	nous vîmes
vous voyiez	vous vîtes
ils/elles voyaient	ils/elles virent

Similar verbs

entrevoir   glimpse
prévoir   foresee; predict
revoir   see again

Notes

1. The future and conditional tenses of **prévoir** are **je prévoirai** and **je prévoirais**, respectively.
2. **Pourvoir** (to provide) is also similarly conjugated: **je pourvoirai** in the future tense; **je pourvoirais** in the conditional; and **je pourvus** in the simple past, **que je pourvusse** in the imperfect subjunctive.

Present participle	Past participle
voyant	vu

Past perfect	Past anterior
j'avais vu	j'eus vu

Future	Future perfect
je verrai	j'aurai vu

Conditional	Conditional perfect
je verrais	j'aurais vu

Present subjunctive	Perfect subjunctive
que je voie	que j'aie vu

Imperfect subjunctive	Pluperfect subjunctive
que je visse	que j'eusse vu

Devant le cinéma

– Tu *as vu* ce film?

– Non. Je vais le *voir* demain.

Outside the movies

– *Have* you *seen* that film?

– No, I'm going to *see* it tomorrow.

A la maison

– Je n'ai pas encore nettoyé la cuisine.

– Ça *se voit!*

At home

– I haven't cleaned the kitchen yet.

– That's *obvious!*

Au musée

– Je suis désolée que vous n'*ayez* pas *vu* l'exposition d'art breton.

– Ça ne fait rien! On la *verra* à Paris.

At the museum

– I'm so sorry you *didn't see* the Breton art exhibit.

– Never mind. We'*ll see it* in Paris.

10k   Vouloir, *to want, wish*
Irregular modal verb in -oir

Imperative

| veuille! (tu) | veuillez! (vous) | voulons! (nous) |

Present	**Perfect**
je veux	j'ai voulu
tu veux	tu as voulu
il/elle veut	il/elle a voulu
on veut	on a voulu
nous voulons	nous avons voulu
vous voulez	vous avez voulu
ils/elles veulent	ils/elles ont voulu

Imperfect	**Simple past**
je voulais	je voulus
tu voulais	tu voulus
il/elle voulait	il/elle voulut
on voulait	on voulut
nous voulions	nous voulûmes
vous vouliez	vous voulûtes
ils/elles voulaient	ils/elles voulurent

Notes

1. This is the only verb of its type, though the patterns of **devoir** and **pouvoir** are similar (➤10b, 10e). Notice that the present indicative tense has irregular forms in the singular and the third-person plural, while the first- and second-persons plural have the stem of the infinitive.

2. The imperative is used as a courtesy in such phrases as **Veuillez agréer, monsieur, l'expression de mes sentiments distingués** (Yours truly); **Veuillez répondre tout de suite** (Please be so good as to reply immediately).

3. Used transitively, **vouloir** means "to want (something)."

Examples of use as a full verb

Tu *veux* une glace?	*Do* you *want* an ice cream cone?
Je *voudrais* cinq kilos de pommes de terre.	I'd *like* five kilos of potatoes.

Present participle	Past participle
voulant	voulu

Past perfect	Past anterior
j'avais voulu	j'eus voulu

Future	Future perfect
je voudrai	j'aurai voulu

Conditional	Conditional perfect
je voudrais	j'aurais voulu

Present subjunctive	Perfect subjunctive
que je veuille	que j'aie voulu
que nous voulions	

Imperfect subjunctive	Pluperfect subjunctive
que je voulusse	que j'eusse voulu

Examples of use as a modal verb

Je *veux* regarder ce film.	I *want* to watch that film.
Il ne *veut* pas aller en Espagne.	He *doesn't want* to go to Spain.
Voulez-vous vérifier la pression des pneus?	*Will* you check the tire pressure?
Voulez-vous me téléphoner ce soir?	*Will* you phone me this evening?
Je *voudrais* voir le chef de personnel.	I*'d like* to see the personnel manager.
Elle ne *veut* rien faire.	She *won't* do a thing.
J'*aurais voulu* assister à leur mariage.	I *would have liked* to go to their wedding.
Jules César *voulut* envahir la Bretagne.	Julius Caesar *wanted* to invade Britain.

C
SUBJECT INDEX

Subject index

The following subjects are covered in PART A, "Verbs in French: their functions and uses,"

D
VERB INDEX

Verb index

There are over 2,200 entries in this section.

Each verb, or verbal expression, is given in French, with its English meaning; a note as to whether it is transitive (tr), intransitive (intr), or reflexive (ref); and its conjugation group.

Verbs that are set out in PART B, "Model French Verbs" are noted ☐M☐.

The thirteen verbs and their compounds that are conjugated with **être** in compound tenses are marked with an asterisk (*). Reflexive verbs are not thus marked, as all reflexive verbs are conjugated with **être** in compound tenses.

Verbs that begin with **h-** are marked ^t**h** if they require no liaison (aspirate h).

Abbreviations: **qch – quelque chose; qqn – quelqu'un.**

A

abandonner (tr)	give up, abandon 7a
abasourdir (tr)	dumbfound, bewilder 8a
abattre (tr)	slaughter 9l
abîmer (tr)	spoil 7a
abolir (tr)	abolish 8a
abonder (intr)	be abundant, abound 7a
abonner, s' (ref)	subscribe 7a
aborder (tr)	reach, approach 7a
aboutir (intr)	work out well 8a
aboutir à (intr)	result in 8a
aboyer (intr)	bark 7f
abriter (tr)	shelter (someone) 7a
abriter, s' (ref)	take shelter 7a
absenter, s' (ref)	be absent, absent oneself 7a
absorber (tr)	take over, absorb 7a
absoudre (tr)	absolve 9r
abstenir de, s' (ref)	keep off, abstain, refrain from 8k
abuser de (tr)	misuse 7a
accélérer (tr & intr)	accelerate 7g
accepter (tr)	agree to, accept 7a
accommoder de qch. s' (ref)	make the best of 7a
accompagner (tr)	accompany 7a
accomplir (tr)	fulfil, achieve 8a

accorder (tr)	grant (request), tune (instrument) 7a
accorder avec, s' (ref)	accord with 7a
accoster (tr)	accost 7a
accoucher de (tr)	give birth to 7a
accouder, s' (ref)	lean (on elbows) 7a
accoupler (tr)	couple 7a
accoupler, s' (ref)	mate 7a
accourir (vers/jusqu'à)(intr)	run to 8d
accrocher (tr)	hook, hang up 7a
accrocher à, s' (ref)	cling to 7a
accroupir, s' (ref)	squat, crouch 8a
accumuler (tr)	accumulate 7a
accuser réception de (tr)	acknowledge (receipt of) 7a
accuser (de) (tr)	accuse, charge (with crime) 7a
acheter (tr)	buy, purchase 7d [M]
acquérir (tr)	acquire, get 8b [M]
acquitter (tr)	acquit 7a
adapter (tr)	adapt 7a
additionner (tr)	add up 7a
adhérer (intr)	adhere, stick to, join 7e
admettre (tr)	admit, grant to be true 9l
administrer (tr)	administer 7a
administrer un médicament (tr)	dose 7a
admirer (tr)	admire 7a
adonner à, s' (ref)	become addicted 7a
adopter (tr)	adopt 7a
adorer (tr)	worship, adore 7a
adosser à, s' (ref)	lean up against 7a
adresser (tr)	address 7a
adresser à, s' (ref)	address 7a
aérer (tr)	air 7e
affaiblir, s' (ref)	weaken 8a
affairer, s' (ref)	bustle 7a
affecter (tr)	affect 7a
affirmer (tr)	affirm 7a
affliger (tr)	afflict, distress 7g
affranchir (tr)	stamp (letters) 8a
affréter (tr)	charter (plane) 7e
affronter (tr)	stand up to 7a
agenouiller, s' (ref)	kneel (down) 7a
aggraver, s' (ref)	get worse 7a
agir (intr)	act, take action 8a
agir de, s' (ref)	be a matter of, be about 8a
il s'agit d'un homme qui . . .	*it's about a man who . . .*

agiter (tr) — wave (flag) 7a
agiter, s' (ref) — get worked up 7a
agrafer (tr) — staple 7a
agrandir (tr) — enlarge 8a
agrandir, s' (ref) — grow larger 8a
aider (tr) — aid, help 7a
aider beaucoup (tr) — do a lot for 7a
aider, s' (ref) — help oneself 7a
aigrir (tr) — sour 8a
aiguiser (tr) — sharpen 7a
aimer (tr) — like, love 7a
ajourner (tr) — adjourn 7a
ajouter (tr) — add, build on (to house) 7a
ajouter (des détails) (tr) — sketch in 7a
alarmer (tr) — alarm 7a
alerter (tr) — alert 7a
aliéner (tr) — alienate 7e
aligner (tr) — align, line up 7a
allaiter (tr) — suckle, breast-feed 7a
alléger (tr) — lighten, alleviate
*aller (intr) — go, suit 7b [M]
  je vais aller (intr) — *I'm going to go*
*aller à la pêche (intr) — go fishing 7b
*aller à l'école (intr) — attend school 7b
*aller à pas furtifs (intr) — go stealthily 7b
*aller à vélo (intr) — go by bike, cycle 7b
*aller au lit (intr) — go to bed 7b
*aller bien (intr) — keep well 7b
*aller chercher (tr) — fetch, go for 7b
*aller de *x* a *y* (intr) — range from *x* to *y* 7b
*aller en bateau (intr) — sail 7b
*aller faire (tr) — go doing 7b
*aller plus vite (intr) — speed up 7b
*aller voir (tr) — go and see, visit 7b
  Allez! (intr) — *Come on!*
  Allons y! (intr) — *Let's go!*
  On y va? (intr) — *Shall we go?*
  Il va jouer au football. — *He's going to play soccer.*
  Comment ça va? (intr) — *How are you?*
  Ça va bien, merci. (intr) — *I'm fine, thanks.*
  Cette robe te va très bien. (intr) — *That dress really suits you.*
  Ça ne va pas du tout. (intr) — *That won't do at all!*
  Ça ira! (intr) — *Things will be ok!*
allier (tr) — ally, combine 7a
allier, s' (ref) — unite with, become allied with 7a

allonger (tr & intr)	stretch, lengthen 7g
allonger, s' (ref)	get longer 7g
allonger la sauce (tr)	thin sauce, "stretch it out" 7g
allouer (tr)	allow, allocate (funds) 7a
allumer (tr)	switch on, ignite, strike a match 7a
allumer, s' (ref)	light up, come on (lights) 7a
alterner (tr)	alternate 7a
amarrer (tr)	moor (boat) 7a
amasser (tr)	hoard 7a
améliorer (tr)	improve, upgrade 7a
amender (tr)	amend 7a
amortir (tr)	deaden, cushion 8a
amplifier (tr)	amplify 7a
amputer (tr)	amputate, cut off 7a
amuser (tr)	amuse 7a
amuser, s' (ref)	play around, have fun, enjoy oneself 7a
analyser (tr)	analyze 7a
anéantir (tr)	annihilate 8a
anesthésier (tr)	anesthetize 7a
animer (tr)	animate 7a
annexer (tr)	annex 7a
annoncer (tr)	announce 7h
annuler (tr)	annul, call off, cancel 7a
anticiper (tr)	anticipate 7a
apercevoir (tr)	sight, spot 10g
apercevoir de, s' (ref)	glimpse, notice 10g
aplanir (tr)	flatten 8a
apparaître (intr)	appear* 9e
appartenir (tr)	belong 8k
appeler (tr)	call, ring up 7c [M]
appeler par radio (tr)	call on the radio 7c
appeler sous les drapeaux (tr)	call up (for military service) 7c
appeler, s' (ref)	be called 7c
applaudir (tr)	clap, applaud 8a
appliquer (tr)	apply 7a
apporter (tr)	bring 7a
apprécier (tr)	enjoy, value 7a
apprendre (tr)	learn 9q
apprendre par coeur (tr)	learn by heart 9q
apprivoiser (tr)	tame 7a
approcher (tr & intr)	close in, bring close 7a
approcher, s' (ref)	approach 7a
approfondir (tr)	deepen 8a
approprier, s' (ref)	appropriate 7a

approuver (tr)	approve 7a
appuyer (tr)	lean (thing) against 7f
appuyer sur (intr)	press 7f
arbitrer (tr)	arbitrate, referee (sport) 7a
argenter (tr)	silver, silver-plate 7a
armer de courage, s' (ref)	steel oneself 7a
armer de, s' (ref)	arm oneself 7a
arranger (tr)	arrange, put in order 7g
arrêter (tr)	stop, stem, arrest 7a
arrêter quelque temps, s' (ref)	stopover (during flight) 7a
arrêter, s' (ref)	stop, draw up (vehicle) 7a
*arriver (intr)	arrive, happen 7a
*arriver à (intr)	get to 7a
arrondir (tr)	round up 8a
arroser (tr)	water 7a
asperger (tr)	sprinkle 7g
aspirer à (tr)	aspire to 7a
assaillir (tr)	assail 8c
assaisonner (tr)	season, flavor 7a
assassiner (tr)	murder, assassinate 7a
assembler (tr)	put together 7a
assembler, s' (ref)	assemble, flock together 7a
asseoir, s' (ref)	sit down, be seated 10a [M]
assiéger (tr)	besiege 7e, 7g
assigner (tr)	assign 7a
assimiler (tr)	assimilate 7a
assister à (intr)	attend, be present at 7a
associer (tr)	associate (something) 7a
associer, s' (ref)	join with, form an alliance 7a
assombrir, s' (ref)	darken 8a
assommer (tr)	knock out 7a
assortir à, s' (ref)	match 8a
assoupir, s' (ref)	doze off 8a
assourdir (tr)	deafen 8a
assujettir (tr)	steady 8a
assurer (tr)	assure, insure, ensure 7a
assurer la liaison avec (tr)	liaise with, get together with 7a
atomiser (tr)	atomize 7a
attacher (tr)	attach, fasten, tie up 7a
attaquer (tr)	attack 7a
atteindre (tr)	attain, arrive at 9o
atteler (tr)	harness 7c
attendre (tr)	wait, expect 9a

attendre avec impatience (tr)	look forward to 9a
attendre à, s' (ref)	expect 9a
atterrir (intr)	land 8a
attirer (tr)	attract, entice 7a
attirer, s' (ref)	incur 7a
attraper (tr)	catch 7a
attrister (tr)	sadden 7a
auditionner (tr)	audition 7a
augmenter (tr)	increase, raise, add to 7a
automatiser (tr)	automate 7a
autoriser (tr)	authorize, entitle 7a
avaler (tr)	swallow 7a
avancer (intr)	move forward 7h
avancer (tr)	advance, further, stick out 7h
avancer à toute vapeur (intr)	steam ahead 7h
avancer, s' (ref)	advance, move forward 7h
aventurer, s' (ref)	venture 7a
avérer, s' (ref)	turn out 7e
avertir (tr)	warn 8a
aveugler (tr)	blind 7a
avoir (tr)	have, have got 6d [M]
il y a (tr)	*there is, are*
Qu'est-ce qu'il y a? (tr)	*What's the matter?*
Il m'a eu. (tr)	*He tricked me (I was had).*
avoir besoin de (tr)	need 6d
avoir chaud (tr)	be hot, feel hot 6d
avoir des rapports avec (tr)	relate to 6d
avoir des rapports (sexuels) avec (tr)	have (sexual) intercourse with 6d
avoir faim (tr)	be hungry 6d
avoir froid (tr)	be cold, feel cold 6d
avoir honte (tr)	be ashamed 6d
avoir la diarrhée (tr)	have diarrhea 6d
avoir l'air (intelligent) (tr)	look (intelligent) 6d
avoir le mal de mer (tr)	be seasick 6d
avoir lieu (tr)	take place 6d
avoir l'intention de (faire) (tr)	intend to (do) 6d
avoir mal au coeur (tr)	feel sick 6d
avoir peur (tr)	be afraid 6d
avoir raison (tr)	be right 6d
avoir sept ans (tr)	be seven years old 6d
avoir soif (tr)	be thirsty 6d
avoir sommeil (tr)	be sleepy 6d
avoir tendance à (tr)	tend 6d
avoir tort (tr)	be wrong 6d

165

	avoir un accident (tr)	have an accident 6d
	avoir un compte à (tr)	bank with, at 6d
	avoir un point de vue (tr)	have a point of view 6d
	avouer (tr)	admit, confess 7a
	bagarrer, se (ref)	brawl 7a
B	**baigner (se)** (tr & ref)	bathe 7a
	bâiller (intr)	yawn, gape 7a
	bâillonner (tr)	gag, stifle 7a
	baiser (tr)	screw (have sex) 7a
	baisser (tr)	lower, come down 7a
	baisser, se (ref)	stoop 7a
	balader, se (ref)	stroll 7a
	balancer (tr)	swing 7h
	balancer, se (ref)	rock 7h
	balayer (tr)	sweep 7i
	bander (tr)	bandage 7a
	bannir (tr)	banish 8a
	baptiser (tr)	baptize 7a
	barrer (tr)	cancel out, cross out 7a
	barrer la porte (tr)	bar 7a
	barricader (tr)	barricade 7a
	baser sur (intr)	base on 7a
	battre (tr)	beat, thresh 9l
	battre du tambour (intr)	beat the drum 9l
	bavarder (intr)	gossip, chat 7a
	baver (intr)	dribble 7a
	bégayer (tr & intr)	stammer 7i
	bêler (intr)	bleat 7a
	bénir (tr)	bless 8a
	bétonner (tr)	concrete over 7a
	beugler (intr)	bellow 7a
	bifurquer (intr)	branch off, fork (road) 7a
	blanchir (tr)	bleach 8a
	blesser (tr)	wound, offend 7a
	blesser, se (ref)	hurt oneself 7a
	bloquer (tr)	block 7a
	blottir, se (ref)	huddle 8a
	bluffer (tr & intr)	bluff 7a
	boire (tr)	drink 9b M
	boire à petits coups (tr)	sip 9b
	boiter (intr)	limp 7a
	bombarder (tr)	bomb, shell 7a
	bomber (intr)	bulge 7a
	bondir (intr)	spring 8a

border (tr)	border 7a
boucher (tr)	cork, plug 7a
bouder (intr)	sulk 7a
bouger (tr & intr)	move, shift 7g
bouillir (intr)	boil 8a
bouillonner (intr)	bubble 7a
bourdonner (intr)	buzz, hum 7a
bourrer (tr)	stuff 7a
bourrer de (tr)	cram with 7a
bousculer, se (tr & ref)	jostle 7a
boutonner (tr)	button 7a
boxer (intr)	box 7a
boycotter (tr)	boycott 7a
braconner (intr)	poach (game) 7a
braiser (tr)	braise 7a
brancher (tr)	connect up to 7a
brasser (tr)	brew 7a
bricoler (tr & intr)	tinker around 7a
brider (tr)	bridle 7a
briller (intr)	shine 7a
broder (tr)	embroider 7a
broncher (intr)	flinch 7a
bronzer, se (ref)	tan 7a
brosser (tr)	brush 7a
brouiller (tr)	blur 7a
brouiller, se (ref)	fall out, quarrel 7a
brouter (tr)	graze 7a
broyer (tr)	grind, crush 7f
brûler (tr)	burn 7a
brûler légèrement (tr)	scorch 7a

C

cabrer se (ref)	rear up 7a
cacher (tr)	hide, conceal 7a
cajoler (tr)	coax 7a
calculer (tr)	calculate, compute 7a
caler (tr & intr)	wedge, stall 7a
câliner (tr)	cuddle, pet 7a
calmer (tr)	calm 7a
calmer, se (ref)	calm down 7a
calomnier (tr)	slander 7a
cambrioler (tr)	burgle 7a
camper (intr)	camp 7a
canaliser (tr)	channel 7a
capituler (intr)	capitulate 7a
capturer (tr)	capture 7a

caractériser (tr)	characterize 7a
caresser (tr)	caress, fondle, stroke 7a
caricaturer (tr)	caricature 7a
carrer (tr)	square 7a
casser (tr)	smash, break 7a
casser net (tr)	snap, break off 7a
cataloguer (tr)	catalog 7a
causer (tr)	cause 7a
céder (tr)	yield, give in, give way 7e [M]
célébrer (tr)	celebrate 7e
censurer (tr)	censor 7a
centraliser (tr)	centralize 7a
centrer (tr)	center on 7a
certifier (tr)	certify 7a
cesser (intr)	stop 7a
cesser de parler (intr)	stop talking 7a
chambrer (tr)	bring to room temperature (wine) 7a
chanceler (intr)	stagger, totter 7c
changer (tr & intr)	change, alter 7g
changer d'avis (tr)	change one's mind 7g
changer de (tr)	switch 7g
changer de sujet (tr)	switch topic 7g
changer de vitesse (tr)	change gear 7g
changer en (intr)	change into 7g
changer, se (ref)	change (clothes) 7g
chanter (intr & tr)	sing 7a
charger (intr)	charge (army) 7g
charmer (tr)	charm 7a
chasser (tr)	chase, hunt, drive 7a
chatouiller (tr)	tickle 7a
chauffer (tr)	warm 7a
chavirer (tr & intr)	capsize 7a
chercher (tr)	look for, search for 7a
chérir (tr)	choose, select 8a
choquer (tr)	shock 7a
chronométrer (tr)	time (race) 7e
chuchoter (tr)	whisper 7a
circuler (tr)	circulate 7a
citer (tr)	quote 7a
clapoter (intr)	lap (waves on shore) 7a
claquer (intr)	bang (of door) 7a
clarifier (tr)	clarify 7a
classer (tr)	class, file 7a
classer, se (tr & ref)	rank 7a

classifier (tr)	classify 7a
cligner des yeux (intr)	wink, blink 7a
cloisonner (tr)	partition off 7a
clôturer (tr)	fence in, enclose 7a
clouer (tr)	nail down 7a
coasser (intr)	croak 7a
cocher (tr)	tick (on list) 7a
coexister (intr)	coexist 7a
cogner contre (intr)	knock against 7a
cohabiter (intr)	cohabit 7a
coincider (intr)	coincide 7a
collaborer (intr)	collaborate 7a
collectionner (tr)	collect 7a
coller (tr)	stick, glue 7a
colorier (tr)	color in 7a
combattre (tr)	fight 9l
combiner (tr)	combine 7a
commander (tr)	order (meal, etc.) 7a
commémorer (tr)	commemorate 7a
commencer (tr)	begin, start, make a start 7h
commettre (tr)	commit 9l
communier (intr)	receive communion 7a
communiquer (tr)	communicate 7a
comparaître (intr)	appear (in court) 9e
comparer (tr)	compare 7a
compiler (tr)	compile 7a
compléter (tr)	complete 7e
complimenter (tr)	compliment 7a
compliquer (tr)	complicate 7a
comploter (tr)	plot 7a
comporter se (tr)	behave 7a
composer (tr)	compose 7a
comprendre (tr)	understand, comprehend 9q
comprimer (tr)	compress 7a
compromettre (tr)	compromise 9l
compter (tr)	count 7a
compter sur (intr)	count on, depend on 7a
concéder (tr)	concede 7e
concentrer (tr)	concentrate 7a
concerner (tr)	concern 7a
concevoir (tr)	conceive, design 10g
conclure (tr)	conclude, close 9c [M]
concourir (tr)	compete, work together 8d
condamner (tr)	damn, condemn, blame 7a
condamner à une amende (tr)	levy a fine 7a
condenser (tr)	condense 7a

coopérer (tr & intr)	cooperate 7e
coordonner (tr)	coordinate 7a
copier (tr)	copy 7a
corder (tr)	string 7a
correspondre (tr)	correspond, write 9a
correspondre à (tr)	correspond to 9a
corriger (tr)	correct 7g
corroder (tr)	corrode 7a
corrompre (tr)	corrupt 9a
coucher, se (ref)	lie down 7a
coudre (tr)	sew,
	stitch 9f ⬜M
couler (tr)	sink 7a
couper (tr)	cut, clip 7a
couper à travers (tr)	cut across 7a
couper la gorge à qqn (tr)	cut someone's throat 7a
couper ras les cheveux (tr)	crop (hair) 7a
courber (tr)	curve, bend 7a
courir (intr)	run, race 8d ⬜M
couronner (tr)	crown 7a
court-circuiter (tr)	short-circuit 7a
coûter (tr)	cost 7a
Ça coute cher.	*It's expensive.*
couver (tr)	hatch 7a
couvrir (tr)	cover 8i
couvrir d'ampoules, se (ref)	blister 8i
couvrir, se (ref)	put on one's hat, cover up;
	cloud over (sky) 8i
couvrir (d'un toit) (tr)	put a roof on 8i
cracher (tr)	spit 7a
crachiner (intr)	drizzle 7a
craindre (tr)	fear 9o
créditer (tr)	credit 7a
créer (tr)	create 7a
crépiter (intr)	crackle 7a
creuser (tr)	dig, sink (a well),
	hollow out 7a
crever (tr)	burst 7d
Je creve de faim!	*I'm starving!*
cribler de (tr)	riddle with 7d
crier (tr)	shout, cry out 7a
cristalliser, se (ref)	crystalize 7a
critiquer (tr)	criticize, censure 7a
croire (tr)	believe, think 9g ⬜M
Je ne crois pas. (tr)	*I don't think so.*
croire en (intr)	believe in 9g

crucifier (tr)	crucify 7a
cuber (tr)	cube 7a
cueillir (tr)	gather, pick 8c [M]
cuire (tr)	cook 9d
cuire à la vapeur/ à feu doux (tr)	steam, simmer 9d
cuisiner (tr)	cook 7a
cultiver (tr)	cultivate, grow, farm 7a

D

daigner (tr)	deign to 7a
danser (tr & intr)	dance 7a
dater de (intr)	date back to 7a
débarquer (tr & intr)	disembark 7a
débarrasser (tr)	clear 7a
débarrasser de, se (ref)	dispose of, get rid of 7a
Elle s'est débarrasée de lui.	*She got rid of him.*
débattre (tr)	debate 9l
débiter qqn d'une somme (tr)	debit 7a
déblayer (tr)	clear away, remove (obstacle) 7i
déborder (tr & intr)	overflow 7a
déboucher (tr)	unblock 7a
débourser (tr)	pay out 7a
déboutonner (tr)	unbutton 7a
débrancher (tr)	disconnect 7a
débrouiller, se (ref)	cope (with) 7a
décerner (tr)	award 7a
décevoir (tr)	disappoint 10g
décharger (tr)	discharge 7g
déchirer (tr)	tear 7a
déchirer, se (ref)	rip, tear, be pulled (muscle) 7a
décider (tr)	decide 7a
décider, se (ref)	make up one's mind 7a
décider pour, se (ref)	decide on 7a
déclarer (tr)	declare 7a
déclarer coupable (tr)	convict, find guilty 7a
déclencher (tr)	trigger off 7a
décoder (tr)	decode 7a
décoller (intr & tr)	take off (plane); unstick 7a
décomposer, se (ref)	decompose 7a
décorer (tr)	decorate 7a
découper (tr)	cut up 7a
découpler (tr)	uncouple 7a
décourager (tr)	discourage 7g

découvrir (tr) — uncover, discover 8i
décréter (tr) — decree 7e
décrire (tr) — describe 9i
décrocher (tr & intr) — take down, lift receiver 7a

dédier (tr) — dedicate 7a
dédommager pour (tr) — compensate for 7g
déduire (tr) — deduce, deduct 9d
défaillir (tr) — faint, falter 8c
défaire (tr) — undo, untie, unpack 9j
défendre (tr) — defend, forbid 9a
défier (tr) — challenge 7a
défiler (intr) — march past, parade 7a
définir (tr) — define 8a
déformer (tr) — distort, deform 7a
dégeler (tr & intr) — thaw 7d
dégivrer (tr) — de-ice, defrost (refrigerator) 7a

dégonfler (tr) — deflate 7a
dégoûter (tr) — disgust 7a
dégoutter (intr) — trickle 7a
dégrader (tr) — degrade, deface 7a
déguiser (se) (tr & ref) — disguise 7a
déjeuner (intr) — have lunch 7a
délayer (tr) — dilute; draw out (a story) 7i
déléguer (tr) — delegate 7e
délibérer (de) (intr & intr) — deliberate 7e
demander (tr) — ask, enquire, request 7a
   Ça demande beaucoup de temps. (tr) — *That takes up a lot of time.*
demander (à qqn de faire qqc) — ask (someone to do something) 7a
demander des nouvelles (tr) — ask after 7a
demander, se (ref) — wonder 7a
démanger (intr) — itch 7g
démaquiller, se (ref) — remove makeup 7a
démarrer (tr & intr) — start 7a
démêler (tr) — disentangle 7a
déménager (intr) — move house 7a
démissionner (intr) — resign 7a
démolir (tr) — demolish 8a
démonter (tr) — take down, dismantle 7a
démontrer (tr) — show, demonstrate 7a
dénigrer (tr) — disparage 7a
dénoncer (tr) — denounce 7h
dénoter (tr) — denote 7a

173

dénoyauter (tr)	stone, pit 7a
dépasser (tr)	surpass, overtake 7a
dépêcher, se (ref)	hurry 7a
Dépéchez-vous! (ref)	*Hurry up!*
dépeindre (tr)	depict 9o
dépenser (tr)	spend 7a
déplacer (tr)	displace 7h
déplaire (tr)	displease 9p
déposer (tr)	deposit, dump 7a
dépouiller (tr)	strip 7a
déprécier (tr)	depreciate 7a
déprimer (tr)	depress 7a
déraisonner (intr)	rave 7a
déranger (tr)	disturb 7g
déraper (intr)	skid 7a
dériver de (tr)	be derived from 7a
dérober, se (ref)	back down 7a
désaltérer, se (ref)	quench 7e
désamorcer (tr)	defuse 7h
désapprouver (tr)	disapprove 7a
désarmer (tr)	disarm 7a
désavouer (tr)	disclaim 7a
*descendre (intr)	come down 7b
descendre (tr)	bring down, carry down 9a
Le gangster l'a descendu. (tr)	*The gangster shot him dead.*
désenivrer (tr & intr)	sober up 7a
déserter (tr)	desert 7a
désespérer, se (ref)	despair 7e
déshabiller (tr)	undress (someone) 7a
déshabiller, se (ref)	get undressed 7a
désherber (tr)	weed 7a
déshériter (tr)	disinherit 7a
désinfecter (tr)	disinfect 7a
désintégrer, se (ref)	disintegrate 7e
désirer (tr)	desire 7a
désorganiser (tr)	disorganize 7a
desservir (tr)	clear away, clear table 8j
dessiner (tr)	draw 7a
détacher (tr)	detach 7a
détacher sur le fond, se (ref)	stand out against (the background) 7a
détailler (tr)	detail 7a
détendre, se (ref)	relax 9a
détériorer (tr)	deteriorate 7a
détériorer, se (ref)	worsen 7a

déterminer (tr)	determine 7a
déterminer la quantité de (tr)	quantify 7a
déterrer (tr)	dig up 7a
détester (tr)	hate 7a
détourner (tr)	divert 7a
détourner un avion (tr)	hijack 7a
détruire (tr)	destroy 9d
dévaliser (tr)	rob 7a
dévaluer (tr)	devalue 7a
dévaster (tr)	devastate 7a
développer (tr)	expand 7a
*devenir (intr)	become 7b
*devenir adulte (intr)	grow up 7b
dévier (tr & intr)	deviate 7a
deviner (tr)	guess 7a
dévisager (tr)	stare at 7g
dévisser (tr)	unscrew 7a
dévisser se (ref)	come unscrewed 7a
devoir (tr)	owe 10b M
devoir (tr)	have to, must 10b
devoir partir (tr)	be called away 10b
dévorer (tr)	devour 7a
diagnostiquer (tr)	diagnose 7a
dicter (tr)	dictate 7a
différencier (tr)	differentiate 7a
différer (intr)	differ 7e
différer de (intr)	be different 7e
digérer (tr)	digest 7e
diluer (tr)	dilute 7a
diminuer (tr & intr)	diminish, lessen 7a
dîner (intr)	dine 7a
dire (tr)	say, tell 9h M
dire au revoir (tr)	say good-bye, see off 9h
dire du mal de (tr)	speak ill of 9h
dire merci (tr)	say thank you 9h
dire, se (ref)	call, be said 9h
Comment ça se dit	*How do you say*
en français?	*that in French?*
diriger (tr)	direct 7g
diriger un orchestre (tr)	conduct orchestra 7g
diriger vers, se (ref)	make for 7g
discerner (tr)	discern 7a
discipliner (tr)	discipline 7a
disculper (tr)	exonerate 7a
discuter (tr & intr)	debate 7a
discuter de (tr)	discuss 7a

disloquer (tr)	disperse 7a
disputer, se (ref)	quarrel, argue 7a
dissiper, se (ref)	wear off 7a
dissoudre (tr)	dissolve 9r
dissoudre, se (ref)	dissolve, be dissolved 9r
dissuader (tr)	dissuade 7a
distiller (tr)	distil 7a
distinguer (tr)	distinguish, tell apart 7a
distraire (tr)	distract 9t
distribuer (tr)	distribute, deal (cards) 7a
diverger (de) (intr)	diverge (from) 7g
diversifier (tr)	diversify, vary 7a
divertir (tr)	entertain 8a
diviser (tr)	divide 7a
diviser en deux (tr)	halve 7a
divorcer (tr)	divorce 7h
divorcer, se (ref)	get divorced 7h
divulguer (tr)	disclose 7a
donner (tr)	give 7a
donner à boire à (tr)	water (animals) 7a
donner à manger à (tr)	feed (animals) 7a
donner de la peine pour, se (tr)	take the trouble to 7a
donner des prévisions météo (tr)	forecast 7a
donner pouvoir à (tr)	commission 7a
donner sur (intr)	open onto, look out on 7a
donner un bain à qqn (tr)	bathe (someone) 7a
donner un coup de pied (tr)	kick 7a
donner un coup de poing (tr)	punch 7a
donner un coup d'oeil (tr)	glance 7a
donner une claque (tr)	smack 7a
doper (tr)	dope 7a
dormir (intr)	sleep 8e ☐M
dormir trop longtemps (intr)	oversleep 8e
doubler (tr)	double 7a
doucher, se (ref)	shower 7a
douter (tr)	doubt 7a
drainer (tr)	drain 7a
dresser (tr)	pitch 7a
dresser une embuscade à (tr)	lie in wait for 7a
dresser, se (ref)	stand up, sit up 7a
droguer (tr)	drug 7a
droguer, se (ref)	take drugs 7a
durcir (tr)	harden 8a
durer (intr)	last, endure, go on 7a

E

éblouir (tr)	dazzle 8a
ébrécher (tr)	chip 7e
écarter de, s' (ref)	get out of way of 7a
échanger (tr)	exchange 7g
échapper à (intr)	slip 7a
échapper de, s' (ref)	escape from 7a
échauffer, s' (ref)	warm up (for sport) 7a
échelonner (tr)	stagger, space out 7a
échouer à (intr)	fail 7a
éclabousser (tr)	splash, spatter 7a
éclaircir, s' (ref)	brighten up, clear up (weather) 8a
économiser (tr)	economize 7a
écorcher (tr)	skin 7a
écosser (tr)	shell 7a
écouter (tr)	listen 7a
écraser (tr)	crush 7a
écraser, s' (ref)	crash 7a
écrire (tr)	write 9i M
écrire pour une demande (tr)	write away for 9i
écrouler, s' (ref)	subside, collapse 7a
éditer (tr)	edit 7a
effacer (tr)	rub out, erase 7h
effleurer (tr)	brush against 7a
effondrer, s' (ref)	flop down 7a
effrayer (tr)	scare, frighten 7i
égaliser (tr)	equalize 7a
égaliser, s' (ref)	even out 7a
égarer, s' (ref)	stray, wander 7a
On s'est égaré. (ref)	*We got lost.*
égoutter, s' (ref)	drip 7a
élaborer (tr)	think out, work out (plan) 7a
élargir (tr)	widen, broaden 8a
électrifier (tr)	electrify 7a
élever (tr)	rear 7d
élever à la puissance *x* (tr)	raise to the power of *x* 7d
élever à, s' (ref)	amount to, add up to 7d
élever une objection contre (tr)	object 7d
éliminer (tr)	eliminate 7a
élire (tr)	elect 9k
éloigner (tr)	move something away from 7a
éloigner, s' (ref)	walk away, move away 7a
emballer (tr)	package 7a
embarquer (tr & intr)	embark 7a

embarrasser (tr)	embarrass, hinder, puzzle 7a
embaucher (tr)	hire, employ 7a
embellir (tr)	embellish 8a
embêter (tr)	annoy 7a
embrasser (tr)	embrace, kiss 7a
embrumer, s' (ref)	become misty 7a
émerger (intr)	emerge from 7g
émettre (tr)	emit, send out 9l
émigrer (intr)	emigrate 7a
emmitoufler, s' (ref)	bundle up 7a
émouvoir (tr)	disturb, upset, move 10f
empaqueter (tr)	wrap up 7a
empêcher (tr)	prevent, hinder 7a
empêcher de s'approcher (tr)	keep away 7a
empêcher de sortir (tr)	keep in 7a
empiffrer, s' (ref)	guzzle 7a
empiler (tr)	pile 7a
empirer (tr)	aggravate, make worse 7a
empirer (intr)	get worse, worsen 7a
employer (tr)	employ, use 7f ☐M☐
empoigner (tr)	grip, grab 7a
empoisonner (tr)	poison 7a
emporter (tr)	carry off, take away 7a
emprisonner (tr)	imprison 7a
emprunter (tr)	borrow 7a
émulsifier (tr)	emulsify 7a
encadrer (tr)	frame 7a
encaisser (tr)	cash 7a
encastrer (tr)	box in, build in 7a
encercler (tr)	encircle 7a
enchaîner (tr)	chain 7a
enchanter (tr)	delight 7a
encourager (tr)	encourage 7g
endommager (tr)	damage 7g
endormir, s' (ref)	go to sleep, fall asleep 8e
endosser (tr)	endorse 7a
enfermer qqn dans (tr)	confine someone to 7a
enfiler (tr)	thread (needle), string (beads) 7a
enflammer (tr)	inflame, set on fire 7a
enflammer, s' (ref)	become inflamed, catch fire 7a
enfoncer (tr)	drive in 7h
enfreindre (tr)	contravene 9o
enfuir, s' (ref)	flee 8g
engager (tr)	hire, involve in 7g

178

E

engager, s' (ref)	commit oneself 7g
engloutir (tr)	gobble 8a
engraisser (tr)	fatten 7a
enivrer, s' (ref)	get drunk 7a
enlever (tr)	remove (clothes), lift, carry off 7d
enlever de sa coquille (tr)	shell 7d
ennuyer (tr)	bore 7f
ennuyer, s' (ref)	be bored, restless 7f
enrayer (tr)	curb, check 7i
enregistrer (tr)	record 7a
enregistrer sur magnéto-scope (tr)	video, record on video 7a
enrhumer, s' (ref)	catch cold 7a
enrichir (tr)	enrich 8a
enrouler (tr)	coil 7a
enseigner (tr)	teach 7a
entasser (tr)	heap, pile up, hoard 7a
entendre (tr)	hear, find out 9a
entendre, s' (ref)	get along with 9a
entendre bien avec, s' (ref)	get on well with 9a
enterrer (tr)	bury 7a
entortiller (tr)	twist 7a
entourer (tr)	surround 7a
entourer d'une haie (tr)	hedge 7a
entraîner (tr)	train 7a
entreprendre (tr)	undertake 9s
***entrer** (intr)	go in, enter 7a
***entrer comme une flèche** (intr)	shoot in 7a
***entrer dans une maison** (intr)	join firm (business) 7a
***entrer en éruption** (intr)	burst in 7a
***entrer en scène** (intr)	come on (stage) 7a
***entrer rapidement** (intr)	sweep in 7a
***entrer par effraction** (intr)	break in, burgle 7a
***entrer dans l'armée** (intr)	join up 7a
entretenir (tr)	maintain, service, provide for 8k
entretenir avec qqn, s' (ref)	confer, converse with 8k
entrouvrir (tr)	half-open 8i
envier (tr)	envy 7a
envoler, s' (ref)	fly away 7a
envoyer (tr)	send 7f
envoyer chercher (tr)	send for, summon 7f
envoyer la facture (tr)	bill 7f
envoyer par téléfax (tr)	fax 7f
envoyer (des suggestions) (tr)	write in 7f

être content (intr)	be pleased 6e
être contrarié (intr)	be annoyed, cross 6e
être contre (intr)	be against 6e
être d'accord (intr)	agree (with), be in agreement 6e
être dans le commerce (intr)	deal 6e
être détaché (intr)	be separate 6e
être dû à (intr)	be due to 6e
être écrivain (intr)	write 6e
être effrayé (intr)	be frightened 6e
être égal (intr)	not to matter 6e
Ça m'est égal. (intr)	*I don't care.* 6e
être en chômage (intr)	be unemployed 6e
être en colère (intr)	be angry 6e
être en expansion (intr)	boom 6e
être en grève (intr)	be on strike 6e
être en retard (intr)	be late 6e
être en séance (intr)	sit, be in session (court, parliament) 6e
être la vedette (intr)	star 6e
être mannequin (intr)	model 6e
être naufragé (intr)	be shipwrecked 6e
être nécessaire (intr)	be necessary 6e
être obligé de (intr)	be obliged to 6e
être parent de (intr)	be related to 6e
être patient/impatient (intr)	be patient/impatient 6e
être permis (intr)	be allowed 6e
être pour/contre (intr)	be for/against 6e
être pris de vertiges (intr)	feel dizzy 6e
être prudent (intr)	be careful 6e
en être quitte pour (intr)	get away with 6e
être reçu (intr)	pass (exam) 6e
être responsable de (intr)	be liable for 6e
être retardé (intr)	be delayed 6e
être retenu (intr)	be delayed 6e
être sage (intr)	behave 6e
être servi de (intr)	be served by 6e
être sur le point de (intr)	be about to 6e
être très impoli envers qqn (intr)	be rude to 6e
être valable (intr)	be valid 6e
étudier (tr)	study 7a
évacuer (tr)	evacuate 7a
évaluer (tr)	appraise 7a
évanouir, s' (ref)	faint 8a
évaporer, s' (ref)	evaporate, boil dry 7a

faciliter (tr)	facilitate 7a
façonner (tr)	fashion, tailor 7a
faillir (intr)	very nearly do,
	just miss doing 8f ☐M
faire (tr)	do, make 9j ☐M
Cela ne fait rien. (tr)	*That doesn't matter.*
faire accepter, se (ref)	get in, on 9j
faire apparaître (tr)	conjure up,
	make appear 9j
faire appel à (tr)	appeal to 9j
faire attention (tr)	pay attention 9j
faire attention à (tr)	attend to 9j
faire attention à qch (tr)	mind, watch out for 9j
faire bouillir (tr)	boil 9j
faire breveter (tr)	patent 9j
faire cadeau de (tr)	give away 9j
faire chanter (tr)	blackmail 9j
faire chauffer (tr)	heat 9j
faire cuire (au four) (tr)	bake 9j
faire de la gymnastique (tr)	do gymnastics 9j
faire de la peine à qqn	upset,
	distress somebody 9j
faire de la publicité (pour) (tr)	advertise 9j
faire de la voile (tr)	go sailing 9j
faire de l'escrime (tr)	fence (sport) 9j
faire de petits travaux (tr)	do odd jobs 9j
faire défiler (tr)	scroll (computer) 9j
faire demi-tour (tr)	turn back 9j
faire des affaires avec (tr)	do business with 9j
faire des courses (tr)	shop, go shopping 9j
faire des progrès (tr)	progress,
	make progress 9j
faire des recherches (tr)	research 9j
faire des signes (tr)	signal 9j
faire désintoxiquer, se (ref)	dry out, come off drugs 9j
faire don de (tr)	donate 9j
faire du bien à (tr)	benefit 9j
faire du bruit (tr)	rattle 9j
faire du commerce (tr)	trade 9j
faire du jogging (tr)	jog 9j
faire du mal à (tr)	hurt, harm 9j
faire du ski (tr)	ski, go skiing 9j
faire du stop (tr)	hitchhike 9j
Il fait du vent. (tr)	*It's windy.* (weather)
faire égoutter (tr)	strain 9j
faire entrer (tr)	show in, let in 9j

faire un régime (tr)	diet 9j
faire remarquer (tr)	remark, comment 9j
faire sauter (tr)	blow up 9j
faire sauter un plomb (tr)	blow a fuse (electrical) 9j
faire semblant de (tr)	pretend 9j
faire signe (tr)	sign 9j
faire signe à qqn (tr)	beckon 9j
faire signe de la main (tr)	wave 9j
faire sortir (tr)	send out 9j
faire suivre (tr)	send on (mail, luggage) 9j
faire sursauter (tr)	startle 9j
faire taire (tr)	silence 9j
faire tort à (tr)	harm 9j
faire un collage (tr)	cut and paste 9j
faire un don à (tr)	give charity 9j
faire un effort (tr)	make an effort 9j
faire un métier (tr)	do (trade, job) 9j
faire un pas (tr)	step 9j
faire un zoom (tr)	zoom 9j
faire une balade (tr)	go for a walk 9j
faire une demande (tr)	apply (for job) 9j
faire une enquête (tr)	carry out an inquiry 9j
faire une entorse, se (ref)	sprain 9j
faire une fausse couche (tr)	miscarry 9j
faire une mise en plis (tr)	set hair 9j
faire une offre de (tr)	bid 9j
faire une ordonnance (tr)	prescribe (medicine) 9j
faire une pause (tr)	pause 9j
faire une promenade (tr)	walk, go for a walk 9j
faire une radio de (tr)	X-ray 9j
faire une randonnée (tr)	ramble 9j
faire une remise de (tr)	discount 9j
faire une valise (tr)	pack 9j
faire voir, se (ref)	show up 9j
falloir (tr)	be necessary 10c [M]
Il ne faut pas fumer!	*You must not smoke!*
faner (intr)	fade 7a
fasciner (tr)	fascinate 7a
fatiguer (tr)	tire 7a
faufiler, se (ref)	slip 7a
favoriser (tr)	favor 7a
fêler (tr)	crack 7a
féliciter (tr)	congratulate 7a
fendre (tr)	split 9a
fermenter (tr & intr)	ferment 7a
fermer (tr)	close, shut 7a

fermer à clef (tr)	lock 7a
fermer à double tour (tr)	double-lock 7a
fermer au verrou (tr)	bolt down 7a
fermer avec une fermeture éclair (tr)	zip 7a
fermer définitivement (tr)	close down 7a
ferrer (tr)	shoe (horse) 7a
fêter (tr)	feast, celebrate 7a
feuilleter (tr)	browse, leaf through 7c
fiancer, se (ref)	get engaged 7h
fier à, se (ref)	trust 7a
filer (tr)	spin 7a
filer (intr)	clear off 7a
filmer (tr)	shoot 7a
filtrer (tr)	filter 7a
financer (tr)	finance 7h
finir (tr)	finish, end, wind up 8a M
finir de travailler (intr)	stop working 8a
fixer (tr)	fix 7a
fixer le prix (tr)	price 7a
flairer (tr)	scent 7a
flamber (intr)	blaze 7a
flâner (intr)	loiter 7a
flatter (tr)	flatter 7a
fleurir (intr)	flower 8a
flirter (intr)	flirt 7a
flotter (intr)	float 7a
fonctionner (intr)	work, function 7a
fonder (tr)	found 7a
fondre (tr)	melt 9a
forcer (tr)	force 7h
formater (tr)	format 7a
former (tr)	form 7a
fouetter (tr)	whip 7a
fouiller (tr)	search 7a
fournir (tr)	supply 8a
fracturer (tr)	fracture 7a
franchir (tr)	clear, get over (barrier), shoot rapids 8a
frapper (tr)	strike 7a
frauder (tr)	defraud 7a
frayer un passage, se (ref)	force one's way 7i
freiner (intr)	brake 7a
frémir (intr)	quiver 8a

fréquenter (tr)	frequent (place), date (person) 7a
friser (tr)	curl 7a
frissonner (intr)	shiver 7a
froisser (tr)	crumple, ruffle 7a
frotter (tr)	rub 7a
frotter au papier de verre (tr)	sandpaper 7a
frustrer (tr)	frustrate 7a
fuir (tr)	flee 8g $\boxed{\text{M}}$
fuire (intr)	leak 9d
fumer (intr)	steam, smoke 7a
fumer (tr)	smoke (cigarettes etc) 7a
fusionner (tr)	merge 7a

G

gâcher (tr)	make a mess of 7a
gagner (tr)	earn 7a
garantir (tr)	guarantee 8a
garder (tr)	guard 7a
garer (tr)	park 7a
gaspiller (tr)	waste 7a
gâter (tr)	spoil 7a
gaver, se (ref)	stuff 7a
gazouiller (intr)	twitter 7a
geler (intr)	freeze 7d
gémir (intr)	moan 8a
gêner (tr)	trouble, embarrass 7a
générer	generate 7e
gérer (tr)	manage 7e
germer (intr)	sprout 7a
gifler (tr)	slap 7a
glacer (tr)	ice 7h
glisser (intr)	slide 7a
gonfler (tr)	inflate 7a
gonfler, se (ref)	swell 7a
goûter (tr)	taste 7a
gouverner (tr)	govern, steer 7a
graisser (tr)	grease 7a
grandir (intr)	grow 8a
gratter (tr)	scrape 7a
graver (tr)	engrave 7a
greffer sur (tr)	graft onto 7a
grêler (intr)	hail 7a
griffer (tr)	scratch 7a
griffonner (tr)	scribble 7a
grignoter (tr)	nibble 7a
griller (tr)	grill 7a

grimper (tr & intr)	climb 7a
grincer (intr)	creak 7h
grisonner (intr)	go gray (hair) 7a
grogner (intr)	growl 7a
gronder (intr)	rumble 7a
grouiller de (intr)	crawl with 7a
grouper, se (ref)	band together 7a
guérir (tr & intr)	heal, cure 8a
guérir, se (ref)	recover, get better 8a
guetter (tr)	look out, lie in wait for 7a
guider (tr)	guide 7a

H

habiller (tr)	clothe 7a
habiller, s' (ref)	get dressed 7a
habiter (tr & intr)	live 7a
habituer (tr)	accustom 7a
habituer, s' (à quelque chose) (ref)	get used to 7a
†**hacher** (tr)	chop 7a
†**haleter** (intr)	gasp 7d
†**handicapper** (tr)	handicap 7a
†**hanter** (tr)	haunt 7a
†**harceler** (tr)	nag 7d
harmoniser (tr)	harmonize 7a
†**hâter de faire, se** (ref)	make haste to do 7a
†**hausser les épaules** (tr)	shrug 7a
†**hausser (le prix)** (tr)	put up (price) 7a
†**hennir** (intr)	neigh 8a
hériter (tr)	inherit 7a
hésiter (intr)	hesitate 7a
†**heurter** (tr)	bump into 7a
†**heurter à** (intr)	bang on, knock at (door) 7a
†**heurter â , se** (ref)	collide with 7a
†**hisser** (tr)	hoist 7a
humecter (tr)	dampen, moisten 7a
humilier (tr)	humiliate 7a
†**hurler** (intr)	howl 7a
hypothéquer (tr)	mortgage 7e

I

idéaliser (tr)	idealize 7a
identifier (tr)	identify 7a
ignorer (tr)	be unaware of 7a
illuminer (tr)	illuminate 7a
illustrer (tr)	illustrate 7a

imaginer (tr)	imagine 7a
imiter (tr)	imitate 7a
immigrer (intr)	immigrate 7a
immuniser (tr)	immunize 7a
importer (intr)	matter 7a
importuner (tr)	molest 7a
impressionner (tr)	impress 7a
imprimer (tr)	print 7a
incinérer (tr)	cremate 7e
inciser (tr)	incise 7a
inciter (tr)	stir 7a
incliner la tête (tr)	nod 7a
incliner, s' (ref)	bend 7a
incorporer (tr)	incorporate 7a
indiquer (tr)	point out/to 7a
infecter (tr)	infect 7a
infecter, s' (ref)	become infected 7a
influencer (tr)	influence 7h
informer (tr)	advise 7a
informer sur, s' (ref)	enquire, get information 7a
ingérer, s' (ref)	interfere, meddle 7e
initier (tr)	initiate 7a
injecter (qch a qqn) (tr)	inject 7a
inonder (tr)	flood 7a
inquiéter (tr)	worry, bother (someone) 7e
inquiéter, s' (ref)	worry 7e
inscrire, s' (à) (ref)	register, enrol (in) 9i
insérer (tr)	insert 7e
insister (intr)	insist 7a
inspirer (tr)	inhale 7a
installer (tr)	sit 7a
installer des micros cachés (tr)	bug 7a
installer, s' (ref)	settle down 7a
instruire (tr)	instruct 9d
insulter (tr)	insult 7a
intégrer (tr)	integrate 7e
intensifier (tr)	intensify 7a
intéresser (tr)	interest 7a
intéresser à, s' (ref)	be interested in 7a
interjeter appel (tr)	lodge an appeal 7c
interpréter (tr)	interpret, read 7e
interroger (tr)	interrogate 7g
interrompre (tr)	interrupt, come in 9a
interrompre son voyage (tr)	stop off (on a trip) 9a

	*intervenir (intr)	intervene, take place, occur 8i
	interviewer (tr)	interview 7a
	intriguer (intr)	scheme 7a
	introduire (tr)	introduce, show in 9d
	introduire progressive-ment (tr)	phase in, introduce gradually 9d
	inventer (tr)	invent 7a
	investir (tr)	invest 8a
	inviter (tr)	invite 7a
	ioniser (tr)	ionize 7a
	irriguer (tr)	irrigate 7a
	irriter (tr)	irritate 7a
	isoler de (tr)	isolate from 7a
J	jardiner (intr)	garden 7a
	jaunir (intr)	turn yellow 8a
	jeter (tr)	throw, cast 7c
	jeter, se (dans) (ref)	plunge into 7c
	jeter un coup d'oeil à (tr)	glance at 7c
	jeter un pont sur (tr)	build a bridge (over a river) 7c
	jeter une bombe (tr)	throw a bomb 7c
	joindre (tr)	connect 9o
	joncher (tr)	strew 7a
	jouer (tr)	gamble, stake 7a
	jouer (tr & intr)	act 7a
	jouer au football (intr)	play soccer 7a
	jouer d'un instrument (intr)	play an instrument 7a
	jouer un rôle (tr)	play a part 7a
	juger (tr)	judge 7g
	jurer (tr)	swear 7a
	justifier (tr)	justify 7a
K	kidnapper (tr)	kidnap 7a
	klaxonner (intr)	blow (car) horn 7a
L	labourer (tr)	till (soil) 7a
	lâcher (tr)	let loose 7a
	laisser (tr)	leave 7a
	laisser entrer (tr)	admit 7a
	laisser passer (tr)	let through 7a
	laisser tomber (tr)	drop 7a

**laisser tromper, ne pas,
se** (ref) see through 7a
  Laissez-moi finir! (tr) *Let me finish!*
lancer (tr) fling 7h
lancer la balle (tr) bowl 7h
languir (intr) pine 8a
larguer les amarres (tr) cast off 7a
larmoyer (intr) snivel, tear up 7f
laver (tr) wash 7a
laver, se (ref) wash self 6c [M]
lécher (tr) lick 7e
légaliser (tr) legalize 7a
léguer (qch à qqn) (tr) leave, bequeath 7e
lever (tr) raise 7d
lever, se (ref) stand up, get up 7d
libérer (tr) set free 7e
lier (tr) bind, tie 7a
lier d'amitié, se (ref) make friends 7a
limer (tr) file 7a
limiter (tr) limit 7a
liquéfier (tr) liquify 7a
lire (tr) read 9k [M]
lire à haute voix (tr) read aloud 9k
lisser (tr) smooth 7a
livrer (tr) deliver 7a
loger (tr) house, accommodate 7g
loucher (intr) squint 7a
louer (tr) rent, hire 7a
louer à bail (tr) lease out 7a
louer une place (tr) reserve, book a seat 7a
lubrifier (tr) oil 7a
luire (intr) gleam 9d
lutter (intr) wrestle 7a

M

mâcher (tr) chew 7a
magnétiser (tr) magnetize 7a
magnétoscoper (tr) video 7a
maigrir (intr) get thin 8a
maintenir (tr) maintain 8k
maintenir, se (ref) keep up 8k
maîtriser (tr) master 7a
mal interpréter (tr) misinterpret 7e
maltraiter (tr) mistreat 7a
manger (tr) eat 7g [M]
manier (tr) handle 7a

mettre au lit, se (ref)	go to bed 9l
mettre au point (tr)	perfect, debug 9l
mettre à, se (ref)	take to, take up 9l
mettre à faire, se (ref)	start to do 9l
mettre à/en (tr)	store 9l
mettre de côté (tr)	put aside, save 9l
mettre en bocal (tr)	bottle 9l
mettre en communication (tr)	put through 9l
mettre en commun (tr)	pool 9l
mettre en faillite (tr)	bankrupt 9l
mettre en pratique (tr)	put into practice 9l
mettre en réserve (tr)	store 9l
mettre en scène (tr)	stage 9l
mettre la table (tr)	lay the table 9l
mettre le feu à (tr)	set fire to 9l
mettre les menottes à (tr)	handcuff 9l
mettre plus fort (tr)	turn up (radio, stereo) 9l
mettre pour la première fois (tr)	wear for first time 9l
mettre qch par écrit (tr)	put down in writing 9l
mettre sur le compte de qqn (tr)	charge (someone's account) 9l
mettre un index (tr)	index 9l
mettre en banque (tr)	bank 9l
miauler (intr)	mew 7a
migrer (intr)	migrate 7a
mimer (tr)	mime 7a
minuter (tr)	time 7a
moderniser (tr)	modernize 7a
modifier (tr)	modify 7a
moisir (intr)	go mouldy 8a
moissonner (tr)	reap 7a
monopoliser (tr)	monopolize 7a
***monter** (intr)	rise 7a
monter (with auxiliary **avoir**) (tr)	take up, carry up 7a
***monter à cheval** (intr)	ride a horse 7a
***monter dans** (intr)	board 7a
***monter d'une classe** (intr)	go up (in school) 7a
***monter en flèche** (intr)	soar 7a
montrer (tr)	show 7a
mordre (tr)	bite 9a
motiver (tr)	motivate 7a
moudre (tr)	mill, grind 9m [M]
mouiller (tr)	wet 7a
mouler (tr)	mold 7a

193

*mourir (intr)   die, pass away 8i M

*mourir de faim (intr)   starve 8i

mousser (intr)   foam, froth 7a

multiplier (tr)   multiply 7a

munir qn de qch (tr)   furnish/equip 8a

mûrir (intr)   ripen 8a

murmurer (tr)   murmur 7a

N   nager (intr)   swim 7g

*naître (intr)   be born 9n M

narrer (tr)   narrate 7a

négliger (tr)   neglect 7g

negocier (tr)   negotiate 7a

neiger (intr)   snow 7g

nettoyer (tr)   clear out 7f

nettoyer à la brosse (tr)   scrub 7f

neutraliser (tr)   neutralize 7a

nicher (se) (intr & ref)   nest 7a

nier (tr)   deny 7a

niveler (tr)   level 7c

noircir (tr)   blacken 8a

nommer (tr)   name, appoint 7a

nommer qn à un poste (tr)   appoint someone to a post 7a

nommer, se (ref)   be called 7a

noter (tr)   note, write down 7a

nouer (tr)   knot 7a

noyer, se (ref)   drown 7f

nuire à (intr)   harm, injure 9d

numéroter (tr)   number 7a

O   obéir à qqn (intr)   obey someone 8b

obliger (tr)   compel 7g

obliquer (tr)   skew 7a

observer (tr)   observe, comply with 7a

obtenir (tr)   obtain, get 8k

occasionner (tr)   bring about 7a

occuper (tr)   occupy (seat), take up 7a

occuper de, s' (ref)   be busy with, concern oneself with 7a

offrir (tr)   offer 8i

ombrager (tr)   shade 7g

omettre (tr)   omit 9l

opérer (tr)   operate 7e

    On l'a opéré. (tr)   *They operated on him.*

opposer (tr)	oppose 7a
opposer à, s' (ref)	confront each other, rebel (against) 7a
orbiter (tr)	orbit 7a
ordonner (tr)	order, ordain 7a
organiser (tr)	organize 7a
osciller (intr)	oscillate 7a
oser (tr)	dare 7a
oublier (tr)	forget, overlook 7a
ouvrir (tr)	open, access a (computer) file 8i [M]
ouvrir sur (intr)	open on to 8i
ouvrir, s' (ref)	open 8i
ouvrir les veines, s' (ref)	slash one's wrists 8i
oxydiser (tr)	oxidize 7a

P

pâlir (intr)	turn pale 8a
palper (tr)	feel 7a
panser (tr)	dress (wound), groom (horse) 7a
paraître (intr)	appear 9e
paralyser (tr)	paralyze 7a
parcourir (tr)	travel across, look through (book) 8d
pardonner (à qqn) (tr)	pardon, forgive someone 7a
paresser (intr)	laze about 7a
parier (tr)	bet 7a
parier sur (intr)	back, gamble on 7a
parler (tr & intr)	speak, talk 7a [M]
parler franchement (intr)	speak candidly 7a
partager (tr)	share, share out 7g
participer à (intr)	take part, join in 7a
*partir (intr)	depart, set off, leave 8j
La fusée est partie. (intr)	*The rocket lifted off.*
*passer (intr)	pass, drop in/by 7a
passer (tr)	pass, hand round 7a
passer au crible (tr)	screen 7a
*passer de mode (intr)	go out of fashion 7a
passer de, se (ref)	dispense with, do without 7a
passer en contrebande (tr)	smuggle 7a
passer en revue (tr)	survey 7a
passer l'aspirateur (tr)	vacuum 7a
*passer par (intr)	go through 7a
passer prendre (tr)	call for 7a
passer, se (ref)	occur 7a

pisser (intr) — piss, urinate 7a
   Son nez pisse le sang. (tr) — *Blood is pouring out of his nose.*

placer (tr) — place 7h [M]
plaindre (tr) — pity 9o
plaindre, se (ref) — complain 9o
plaire (à qqn) (intr) — please (someone) 9p [M]
plaisanter (intr) — joke, have a joke 7a
planer (intr) — glide 7a
planter (tr) — plant 7a
plâtrer (tr) — plaster 7a
pleurer (intr) — weep, cry 7a
pleuvoir (intr) — rain 10d [M]
plier (tr) — fold 7a
plisser (tr) — pleat 7a
plomber (tr) — seal, fill (tooth) 7a
plonger (tr & intr) — plunge 7g
poignarder (tr) — stab 7a
poinçonner (tr) — punch 7a
pointer à la sortie (intr) — clock out 7a
pointer à l'arrivée (intr) — clock in 7a
poivrer (tr) — pepper 7a
polir (tr) — polish, shine 8a
polluer (tr) — pollute 7a
polycopier (tr) — photocopy 7a
pomper (tr) — pump 7a
pondre (tr) — lay 9a
porter (tr) — wear, carry 7a
porter un toast à (tr) — toast (in champagne, etc) 7a

porter des fruits (tr) — bear fruit 7a
poser (tr) — fit 7a
poser une question (tr) — ask a question 7a
posséder (tr) — possess 7e
poster (tr) — mail 7a
potasser (intr) — study (hard), cram 7a
poudrer (tr) — powder 7a
pouffer de rire (intr) — giggle 7a
pourchasser (tr) — pursue 7a
pourrir (intr) — rot 8a
poursuivre (tr) — follow up 9u
poursuivre en justice (tr) — prosecute 9u
pourvoir (de) (tr) — provide (with) 10j
pourvoir en personnel (tr) — staff 10j
pousser (tr) — shove 7a

prétendre (tr)	allege 9a
prêter (tr)	lend 7a
prévaloir (sur) (intr)	prevail (over) 10i
prévoir (tr)	forecast 10j
prier (tr)	pray, beg 7a
priser (tr)	prize 7a
privatiser (tr)	privatize 7a
priver de, se (ref)	go without 7a
procéder (intr)	proceed 7e
procréer (tr)	procreate 7a
produire (tr)	produce 9d
profiter de (intr)	profit (from) 7a
profiter à (intr)	benefit (someone) 7a
programmer (tr)	program 7a
projeter (tr)	project 7c
prolonger (tr)	prolong 7g
promener (tr)	take for a walk 7d
promener se (ref)	go for a walk 7d
promettre (tr)	promise 9l
promouvoir (tr)	promote 10f [M]
prononcer (tr)	pronounce 7h
prononcer une	
condamnation (tr)	convict, sentence 7h
proposer (tr)	propose 7a
prospérer (intr)	thrive 7e
prostituer, se (ref)	prostitute oneself 7a
protéger (tr)	protect 7e/7g
protester (tr)	protest 7a
prouver (tr)	prove 7a
publier (tr)	issue 7a
puer (tr)	stink 7a
puiser (tr)	draw (water, resources) 7a
pulvériser (tr)	grind 7a
punir (tr)	punish 8a
purifier (tr)	purify 7a

Q

qualifier (tr)	qualify 7a
questionner (tr)	question, interrogate 7a

R

raccourcir (tr)	shorten 8a
raccourcir, se (ref)	become shorter 8a
raccrocher (intr)	hang up (the telephone) 7a
raconter (tr)	tell, relate (a story) 7a
radiodiffuser (tr)	broadcast 7a

recopier (tr)	write out 7a
recoucher (tr)	put back to bed 7a
recourir à (intr)	resort to,
	have recourse to 7c
recouvrer (tr)	recover, regain 7a
recouvrir (tr)	cover over,
	cover again, hide 8i
rectifier (tr)	rectify 7a
reculer (intr)	reverse, move back 7a
recupérer (tr)	salvage get back 7e
recycler (tr)	recycle 7a
rédiger (tr)	draw up, draft 7g
rédiger le compte-rendu (tr)	draft the report 7g
redoubler (tr)	increase, redouble;
	repeat year at school 7a
redouter (tr)	dread 7a
redresser (tr)	straighten, set upright 7a
redresser, se (ref)	sit up 7a
réduire (tr)	reduce, cut down 9d
réduire en esclavage (tr)	enslave 9d
refaire (tr)	redo 9j
refaire qqn de qch (tr)	do out of 9j
réfléchir (intr)	reflect 8a
réfléchir à (intr)	think over 8a
refléter (tr)	reflect (light) 7a
réfrigérer (tr)	refrigerate 7e
refroidir (tr)	cool down 8a
refuser (tr)	turn down 7a
réfuter (tr)	refute 7a
regarder (tr)	look at, watch 7a
regarder fixement (tr)	stare at, gaze at 7a
régler (tr)	settle 7e
régler sa note (tr)	check out, pay bill 7e
regretter (tr)	be sorry 7a
rejeter (tr)	reject 7c
rejoindre (tr)	rejoin 9o
rejoindre, se (ref)	link up 9o
réjouir, se (ref)	rejoice 8a
relâcher (tr)	loosen, slacken 7a
relayer (tr)	relay 7i
relever (tr)	lift, heighten 7d
remarquer (tr)	remark, notice 7a
rembobiner (tr)	rewind (cassette) 7a
rembourser (tr)	reimburse 7a
remercier (tr)	thank 7a
remettre à (tr)	hand over 9l

INDEX

reprendre la forme (tr)	get fit 9q
représenter (tr)	represent, stand for 7a
réprimander (tr)	scold 7a
reprocher (tr)	reproach 7a
reproduire (tr)	reproduce 9d
réserver (tr)	reserve, book 7a
resister à (intr)	resist 7a
résonner (intr)	resonate, echo 7a
résoudre (tr)	resolve, work out 9r M
résoudre, se (ref)	decide,
	make up one's mind 9r
respecter (tr)	respect 7a
respirer (tr & intr)	breathe 7a
ressembler à (intr)	take after 7a
resserrer (tr)	tighten 7a
*ressortir (intr)	stand out 8j
restaurer (tr)	restore 7a
*rester (intr)	stay 7a
*rester à jeun (intr)	fast 7a
*rester en arrière (intr)	stop behind, drop back 7a
*rester là (intr)	stand by 7a
résulter de (intr)	result from 7a
résumer (tr)	summarize 7a
retarder (tr & intr)	delay, be slow (clock) 7a
retenir (tr)	hold back, detain 8k
retentir (intr)	blare, echo 8a
retirer (tr)	draw out 7a
retirer, se (ref)	withdraw 7a
retourner (tr)	turn upside down 7a
*retourner (intr)	return, go back 7a
retourner, se (ref)	turn round 7a
rétrécir (tr)	shrink 8a
rétrécir, se (ref)	narrow 8a
retrouver (tr)	find again, meet 7a
retrouver, se (ref)	meet each other
	(arranged) 7a
réunir (tr)	reunite, amalgamate 8a
réussir (intr)	succeed,
	take off (project) 8a
réussir à (intr)	succeed in, pass (exam) 8a
réussir à faire (tr)	manage to do,
	succeed in doing 8a
revaloir (tr)	pay back, get even 10i
rêvasser (intr)	daydream 7a
réveiller (tr)	wake (someone) 7a
réveiller, se (ref)	wake up 7a

savoir (tr)	know 10h $\boxed{\text{M}}$
savoir nager (intr)	know how, be able to swim 10h
savonner (tr)	soap 7a
savourer (tr)	savor 7a
sceller (tr)	seal 7a
sécher (tr)	dry 7e
sécher les cours (tr)	skip classes 7e
secouer (tr)	shake 7a
secourir (tr)	help, assist 8d
séduire (tr)	seduce 9d
séjourner (intr)	stay 7a
sélectionner (tr)	select 7a
seller (tr)	saddle 7a
sembler (intr)	look (seem) 7a
semer (tr)	sow 7d
sentir (tr & intr)	feel, sense, smell 8j $\boxed{\text{M}}$
sentir, se (ref)	feel 8j
séparer (tr)	separate 7a
séparer de (tr)	separate from 7a
séparer de, se (ref)	part (company) 7a
serrer (tr)	clamp 7a
servir (tr)	serve; bowl (sport) 8j
servir à boire (tr)	serve drinks 8j
servir à (+ infinitive) (intr)	serve to, be used for 8j
servir de, se (ref)	use 8j
servir de (intr)	put to use as 8j
shooter (intr)	shoot (soccer) 7a
shooter, se (ref)	inject oneself with drugs 7a
siffler (intr)	hiss, whistle 7a
signer (tr)	sign 7a
signer, se (ref)	cross oneself 7a
signifier (tr)	mean 7a
situer, se (ref)	be located 7a
soigner (tr)	care for 7a
solder (tr)	sell cheap 7a
solidifier (tr)	solidify 7a
songer (tr & intr)	dream, think 6b
sonner (intr)	sound 7a
sonner l'heure (tr)	chime 7a
sortir (tr)	bring out 8j
***sortir** (intr)	go out 8a
***sortir comme un ouragan** (intr)	storm out 8a
***sortir comme une flèche** (intr)	dart out 8j
***sortir de** (intr)	go out of 8j
soucier de, se (ref)	care about 7a

souder (tr)	weld 7a
souffler (intr)	blow 7a
souffrir (intr)	suffer 8i
souffrir de (intr)	suffer from 8i
souhaiter (tr)	wish, wish for, long for 7a
souhaiter la bienvenue à (tr)	welcome 7a
soulager (tr)	relieve 7g
soulever (tr)	raise 7d
soulever, se (ref)	rise 7d
souligner (tr)	underline, emphasize 7a
soumettre (tr)	subject 9l
soumettre, se (ref)	submit 9l
soumettre à, se (ref)	abide by (rules) 9l
soupçonner (tr)	suspect 7a
soupirer (intr)	sigh 7a
soupirer après (intr)	pine for 7a
sourire (intr)	smile 9s
soustraire (tr)	subtract 9t ⬜M
soutenir (tr)	uphold, stand by 8k
spécialiser, se (en) (ref)	specialize (in) 7a
spécifier (tr)	specify 7a
spéculer (intr)	speculate 7a
squatter (intr)	squat (occupy illegally) 7a
stabiliser (tr)	stabilize 7a
standardiser (tr)	standardize 7a
stationner (tr)	park (vehicle) 7a
structurer (tr)	structure 7a
stupéfier (tr)	stupefy 7a
subir (tr)	suffer 8a
suborner (tr)	bribe 7a
subsister de (intr)	live on 7a
subventionner (tr)	subsidize 7a
succéder à qqn (intr)	succeed someone 7e
sucer (tr)	suck 7h
sucrer (tr)	sweeten, sugar 7a
suer (intr)	sweat 7a
suffire (intr)	be sufficient 6c
Ça suffit!	*That's enough!*
suffoquer (tr & intr)	suffocate 7a
suggérer (tr)	suggest 7e
suinter (intr)	ooze, seep 7a
suivre (tr & intr)	follow, come after 9u ⬜M
suivre la trace de (tr)	track, trace 9u
suivre son petit traintrain (tr)	potter about 9u
suivre un conseil (tr)	act on advice 9u
supplier qqn de (tr)	beg 7a

supporter (tr)	stand, bear 7a
supposer (intr)	suppose 7a
supprimer (tr)	cut out 7a
surgir (intr)	pop up 8a
surpasser (tr)	surpass 7a
surplomber (intr)	overhang 7a
surprendre (tr)	surprise 9q
sursauter (intr)	start 7a
surveiller (tr)	supervise 7a
survivre (intr)	survive 9v
survivre a qqn (intr)	outlive someone 9v
suspendre (tr)	suspend 9a
synthétiser (tr)	synthesize 7a

T

tabasser (tr)	beat someone up 7a
tacher (tr)	spot, dirty 7a
tailler (tr)	prune 7a
taire, se (ref)	be silent 9p
tambouriner (tr & intr)	drum 7a
tamiser (tr)	sieve 7a
taper (tr & intr)	hit, beat 7a
taper à la machine (tr)	type 7a
Il tape soixante mots par minute. (tr)	*He types sixty words per minute.*
taper du pied (intr)	stamp 7a
taper sur les nerfs de qqn (intr)	get on someone's nerves 7a
tapir, se (ref)	cower 8a
tapisser les murs (tr)	hang wallpaper 7a
tapoter (tr & intr)	tap 7a
taquiner (tr)	tease 7a
taxer (tr)	tax 7a
téléphoner (qch, à qqn) (tr)	telephone 7a
témoigner (intr)	witness, testify 7a
témoigner de qch (tr)	bear witness to 7a
tendre (tr)	stretch, hold out, offer 9a
tendre une embuscade (tr)	ambush 9a
tenir (tr & intr)	hold 8k [M]
Tiens! (intr)	*Really! Well!*
tenir bon (intr)	hold one's own 8k
tenir compte de (tr)	take into account, allow for 8k
tenir le coup (tr)	bear up 8k
tenir, se (ref)	stand 8k
tenter (tr)	tempt 7a

terminer (tr)	finish off, end 7a
terminer en pointe (intr)	taper 7a
terrifier (tr)	terrify 7a
terroriser (tr)	terrorize 7a
tirer (tr)	pull, draw, shoot 7a
Il a tiré plusieurs coups de feu. (tr)	*He fired several shots.*
tirer des exemplaires (tr)	duplicate, run off copies 7a
tirer sans gains ni pertes, s'en (intr)	break even 7a
tisser (tr)	weave 7a
tolérer (tr)	tolerate, put up with 7e
***tomber** (intr)	fall 6b [M]
***tomber amoureux** (intr)	fall in love 6b
***tomber en panne** (intr)	break down 6b
***tomber malade** (intr)	fall ill 6b
tondre (tr)	shear 9a
tondre le gazon (tr)	mow the lawn 9a
tonner (intr)	thunder 7a
tordre (tr)	wring 9a
tordre, se (la cheville) (ref)	twist (ankle) 9a
torturer (tr)	torture 7a
toucher (tr)	touch, press; receive (money) 7a
tourner (tr & intr)	turn 7a
tousser (intr)	cough 7a
tracasser (tr)	worry, play up 7a
traduire (tr)	translate 9d
trahir (tr)	betray 8a
traîner (intr)	linger 7a
traire (tr)	milk (cow) 9t
traiter (tr)	treat 7a
traiter le texte (tr)	word-process 7a
trancher (tr)	slice 7a
transcrire (tr)	transcribe 9i
transférer (tr)	transfer, download (IT) 7e
transformer (tr)	transform 7a
transmettre (tr)	pass down 9l
transporter (tr)	transport, ship 7a
traquer (tr)	hound 7a
travailler (intr)	work 7a
travailler au noir (intr)	moonlight 7a
travailler bien (intr)	work hard, get on with 7a
travailler comme un forcené (intr)	work like mad 7a
travailler dur (intr)	work hard 7a

traverser (tr)	go across, cross 7a
trébucher (intr)	trip, stumble 7a
trembler (intr)	tremble 7a
tremper (tr)	soak, steep, dip 7a
tresser (tr)	twine, braid 7a
tricher (intr)	cheat 7a
tricoter (tr)	knit 7a
trier (tr)	sort 7a
tromper (tr)	mislead 7a
tromper, se (ref)	be mistaken 7a
trouver (tr)	find 7a
trouver, se (ref)	be found, be 7a
trouver à redire à (tr)	object to 7a
tuer (tr)	kill 7a
tutoyer (se) (tr & ref)	say "**tu**" (address informally) 7f
tyranniser (tr)	bully 7a

U

unir (tr)	unite 8a
unir, s' (ref)	bond 8a
uriner (intr)	urinate 7a
user (tr)	wear out 7a
user, s' (ref)	wear out, become worn out 7a
utiliser (tr)	use 7a

V

vaciller (intr)	flicker 7a
vaincre (tr)	overcome 9v [M]
valoir (intr)	be worth 10i [M]
vanter, se (ref)	boast, brag 7a
vaporiser (tr)	spray 7a
vaporiser, se (ref)	vaporize 7a
varier (tr)	vary 7a
vendre (tr)	sell 9a [M]
vendre au détail (tr)	retail 9a
vénérer (tr)	worship, revere 7e
*venir (intr)	come 8k
venez vous asseoir auprés de nous	*come and join us, come sit with us*
*venir à échéance (intr)	fall due 8k
*venir à l'esprit (intr)	occur 8k
*venir de Rome (intr)	come from Rome 8k
*venir de faire (intr)	have just done 8k
*venir voir (tr)	come and see, come round 8k